UNDERSTANDING
Theodore Roethke

Understanding Contemporary
American Literature

Matthew J. Bruccoli, *Editor*

UNDERSTANDING
Theodore
ROETHKE

BY WALTER B. KALAIDJIAN

UNIVERSITY OF SOUTH CAROLINA PRESS

Published in Columbia, South Carolina, by the
University of South Carolina Press

Manufactured in the United States of America

Library of Congress Cataloging-in-Publication Data

Kalaidjian, Walter B., 1952–
  Understanding Theodore Roethke.

  (Understanding contemporary American literature)
  Bibliography: p.
  Includes index.
  1. Roethke, Theodore, 1908–1963—Criticism and
interpretation. I. Title. II. Series.
PS3535.039Z65   1987   811'.54   87-3476
ISBN 0-87249-513-2
ISBN 0-87249-514-0 (pbk.)

CONTENTS

For
Emily, Willa, and Andrew

EDITOR'S PREFACE

Understanding Contemporary American Literature has been planned as a series of guides or companions for students as well as good nonacademic readers. The editor and publisher perceive a need for these volumes because much of the influential contemporary literature makes special demands. Uninitiated readers encounter difficulty in approaching works that depart from the traditional forms and techniques of prose and poetry. Literature relies on conventions, but the conventions keep evolving; new writers form their own conventions—which in time may become familiar. Put simply, *UCAL* provides instruction in how to read certain contemporary writers—identifying and explicating their material, themes, use of language, point of view, structures, symbolism, and responses to experience.

The word *understanding* in the series title was deliberately chosen. Many willing readers lack an adequate understanding of how contemporary literature works; that is, what the author is attempting to express and the means by which it is conveyed. Although the criticism and analysis in the series have been aimed at a level of general accessibility, these introductory volumes are meant to be applied in conjunction with the works they cover. Thus they do not provide a substitute for the works and authors they introduce, but rather prepare the reader for more profitable literary experiences.

M. J. B.

ACKNOWLEDGMENTS

Several colleagues were helpful in bringing *Understanding Theodore Roethke* to fruition. I wish to thank Cary Nelson at Illinois for early direction in my writing about Roethke and Matthew J. Bruccoli for much appreciated advice in the advanced stages of this project. Randall Stiffler provided useful consultation in participating with me on a Modern Language Association panel devoted to Roethke. In addition, I want to thank Mercer University for providing released time from my teaching duties and summer research support. Finally, I gratefully acknowledge permission to quote from the following:

"The Dance," Copyright 1952 by the Atlantic Monthly Company; "His Words," "The Exulting," "The Wall," "What Now?" Copyright © 1956 by Atlantic Monthly Co., *Yale Review, The American Scholar*; "Big Wind," Copyright 1947 by The United Chapters of Phi Beta Kappa, The New Republic; "Weed Puller," Copyright 1946 by Editorial Publications, Inc.; "Elegy," "Love's Progress," "The Shimmer of Evil," Copyright © 1955 by New Republic, Inc., *The Virginia Quarterly Review, The Commonweal*; "A Field of Light," Copyright 1947 by The Tiger's Eye, *The Sewanee Review*; "My Papa's Waltz," Copyright 1942 by Hearst Magazines, Inc.; "Old Florist," Copyright 1946 by Harper & Brothers, *American Mercury*; "I Waited," Copyright © 1956 by Kenyon College.

All other poems from *The Collected Poems of*

ACKNOWLEDGMENTS

Theodore Roethke Copyright © 1982 by Beatrice Roethke, Administratix of the Estate of Theodore Roethke, reprinted by permission of Doubleday & Company, Inc., and Faber and Faber, Ltd. All selections from *On the Poet and His Craft: Selected Prose of Theodore Roethke*, ed. Ralph J. Mills, Jr. (Copyright © 1965 by Beatrice Roethke as administratrix of the estate of Theodore Roethke).

"The Lovesong of J. Alfred Prufrock," *The Waste Land*, "East Coker," "Little Gidding," and "Burnt Norton," by T. S. Eliot, *The Complete Poems, 1909–1962* (Copyright 1971 by Harcourt Brace Jovanovich, Inc. and Faber and Faber, Ltd.).

"The Magi," (Copyright 1916 by Macmillan Publishing Company, renewed 1944 by Bertha Georgie Yeats); "The Hawk," (Copyright 1919 by Macmillan Publishing Company, renewed 1947 by Bertha Georgie Yeats); "The Second Coming," (Copyright 1924 by Macmillan Publishing Company, renewed 1952 by Bertha Georgie Yeats); "The Tower" and "Leda and the Swan" (Copyright 1928 by Macmillan Publishing Company, renewed 1956 by Georgie Yeats); "Vacillation," "Byzantium," and "Crazy Jane Talks with the Bishop" (Copyright 1933 by Macmillan Publishing Company, renewed 1961 by Bertha Georgie Yeats) in *The Variorum Edition of the Poems of W. B. Yeats*, edited by Peter Allt and Russell K. Alspach, with world-

ACKNOWLEDGMENTS

wide rights granted by A. P. Watt, Ltd.

"Song of Myself," Walt Whitman, *Poetry and Prose* (Copyright 1982 by The Library of America).

Reprinted from W. J. B. Owen (ed.): *The Fourteen-Book "Prelude,"* by William Wordsworth, Copyright © 1985 by Cornell University. Used by permission of the publisher, Cornell University Press.

"My Heart Leaps Up," reprinted from Jared Curtis (ed.): *"Poems, in Two Volumes," and Other Poems*, 1800–1807, by William Wordsworth. Copyright © 1983 by Cornell University Press. Used by permission of the publisher.

"Sunday Morning," by Wallace Stevens, *The Palm at the End of the Mind*, ed. Holly Stevens (Copyright 1971 by Alfred A. Knopf, Inc.).

UNDERSTANDING
Theodore Roethke

CHAPTER ONE

Understanding
Theodore Roethke

Like other major postwar poets, Robert Lowell and John Berryman, for example, Theodore Roethke's verse was shaped by autobiographical themes and key events from his personal life. A basic knowledge of the poet's career, therefore, is important for understanding his writing. Born in 1908 to German-American parents, Roethke spent his childhood and adolescence in the rural setting of Saginaw, Michigan. His grandfather Wilhelm had emigrated from Prussia in 1870. In America the Roethke family managed a prosperous greenhouse business that was passed on to Roethke's father, Otto. Saginaw's regional landscape and the family greenhouses profoundly shaped Roethke's imaginative vision throughout his career. As a student at Saginaw's Arthur Hill High School, Roethke showed early promise in literature, creative writing, and public speaking. These formative years, however, were marked by family turmoil culminating in the sale of the green-house business in 1922, and in his uncle's suicide and Otto's death from cancer in 1923.

Roethke enjoyed academic success as an undergraduate at the University of Michigan at Ann Arbor (1925–29), graduating *magna cum laude* and a member of Phi Beta Kappa. Although urged by his family to pursue a legal career, he quit law school after only one semester, turning instead to English studies. From 1929–31, Roethke took graduate courses at the university of Michigan and later the Harvard Graduate School, where he worked closely with Robert Hillyer. The Depression years cut short Roethke's graduate work, and out of economic necessity he took up an academic career first at Lafayette College from 1931–35, followed by positions at Michigan State University (1935), Pennsylvania State College (1936–43), Bennington College (1943–46), and finally the University of Washington from 1947 until his death in 1963.

During the mid-1930s, Roethke enjoyed a growing reputation as a poet—publishing in such prestigious journals as *Poetry*, the *New Republic*, the *Saturday Review*, and *Sewanee Review*. In the midst of this early success, Roethke was hospitalized at Ann Arbor's Mercywood sanitarium in 1935 for what would prove to be recurring bouts of mental illness. Roethke viewed these periodic incidents of manic depression as opportunities for creative self-exploration, allowing him as he said to "reach a new level of reality" by following Rimbaud's program of *dérèglement de tous les sens*.[1]

The 1940s and '50s were decades of steady ascendancy in Roethke's poetic and academic careers. With the editorial advice of Stanley Kunitz, Roethke assembled his first volume of poetry *Open House* (1941) published by Alfred A. Knopf. The next year the poet was invited to give one of the prestigious Morris Gray lectures at Harvard, and a Guggenheim Fellowship followed in 1945. At Bennington, Roethke struck an alliance with Kenneth Burke, who offered critical advice and support for Roethke's "greenhouse" poems, later included in *The Lost Son and Other Poems* (1948). A second Guggenheim Fellowship in 1950 allowed him time to finish his third volume *Praise to the End!* leading to major grants from the Ford Foundation and National Institute of Arts and Letters in 1952. At this time, Roethke resumed his relationship with Beatrice O'Connell, whom he had known earlier from his years at Bennington. The two were married in January 1953 and spent March through August in Europe. From here Roethke edited the galley proofs of *The Waking* (1953), which won the Pulitzer Prize in 1954. Roethke spent the following year in Italy as a Fulbright lecturer. But there was trouble ahead, and 1957 was a difficult year with Beatrice convalescing from tuburculosis and Roethke hospitalized at Halcyon House Sanitarium for another of his manic incidents. Roethke received a generous award from the Chapelbrook Foundation in 1958, and that same year Doubleday published *Words for the Wind*, for which he received a National Book Award, the Bollingen Prize, Edna St. Vincent Millay Prize, the Longview Foundation Award, and the Pacific Northwest Writer's Award.

The last four years of the poet's life were among his most prolific, culminating in the publication of sixty-one new poems along with several long works that were published posthumously in *The Far Field* (1964)—winner of a National Book Award—and *The Collected Poems* (1966). In addition to several reading tours, Roethke traveled extensively in Europe on a two-year Ford Foundation Grant from 1959–61. *Party at the Zoo* a book of children's verse, and *Sequence Sometimes Metaphysical* were published in 1963. On August 1, that year Roethke suffered a fatal heart attack while visiting with friends at Bainbridge Island, Washington.

Overview

James Dickey confirmed Roethke's importance to contemporary letters, dubbing him "The Great-

OVERVIEW

est American Poet" in a 1968 review of Allan
Seager's biography of the poet, *The Glass House*.
The title of Dickey's review, however respectful,
ironically alluded to the poet's well-known obsession with possessing that central position in the
American canon. As Seager has discussed, the
poet carried on a shrewd and tireless campaign to
promote his literary reputation, lobbying important editors, other writers, grant officers, and
award foundations. Even as Roethke began to hit
his stride with the publication of his second volume *The Lost Son and Other Poems* (1948), he was
plagued by anxieties that his writing was already
belated, for at this time the postwar literary milieu
was dominated by the powerful poetic achievements of the major High Modernist writers. As
Charles Molesworth has observed, Roethke's early
writings emerged at a time when the careers of the
major High Modernists were climaxing in such
masterpieces as Yeats's *Last Poems* (1940), Eliot's
Four Quartets (1943), Stevens's *Transport to Summer*
(1947), and Pound's *Pisan Cantos* (1948). It was a
period too whose literary tastes were being shaped
by John Crowe Ransom in *The World's Body* (1938)
and *The New Criticism* (1941).[2] Throughout his
career, Roethke acknowledged both his respect for
and rivalry with his "spiritual ancestors" and "Supreme Masters": T. S. Eliot, Wallace Stevens, Walt
Whitman, and W. B. Yeats.

As several of Roethke's critics have discussed, his self-conscious relation to literary predecessors comprises only one aspect of his poetry's confessional dimension. It stands as the public and professional counterpart to the poet's private relation to his father, Otto, whose death from cancer profoundly affected Roethke's adolescence. The loss of the father is the central subject of *The Lost Son* and persists as a psychological narrative throughout Roethke's confessional works. Karl Malkoff, in particular, has argued cogently that Roethke's ambivalence toward his literary "fathers" parallels his need to reconcile himself to Otto's untimely death.[3] Indeed, Roethke himself in a telling essay entitled "How to Write Like Somebody Else" described his uneasy relation to Yeats in terms of "daring to compete with papa."[4] Elsewhere, the poet explicitly joined these two confessional themes as complementary aspects in his struggle for personal and literary identity: "In any quest for identity today—or any day—we run up inevitably against this problem: What to do with our ancestors? I mean it as an ambiguity: both the literal or blood, and the spiritual ancestors. Both, as we know, can overwhelm us. The devouring mother, the furious papa. And if we're trying to write, the Supreme Masters" (PC, 23). During the postwar decades, then, Roethke's poetics developed

OVERVIEW

through an exploration of personal identity: a confessional exchange between, on the one hand, his professional roles of poet, teacher, and critic, and on the other, his private encounters with a deeper "individuated" self.

In a 1963 address "On Identity," delivered at Northwestern University, Roethke discussed his principle concern for identity in terms of four major themes: "(1) The multiplicity, the chaos of modern life; (2) The way, the means of establishing a personal identity, a self in the face of that chaos; (3) The nature of creation, that faculty for producing order out of disorder in the arts, particularly in poetry; and (4) The nature of God Himself" (PC, 19). From the very beginning of his career, Roethke takes up the challenge of asserting identity in the midst of modernity both aesthetically and spiritually. Roethke's first volume *Open House* stages the confessional drama of the poet's struggle to achieve personal and literary identity. Works such as "Feud," "Prognosis," "Prayer," and "Reply to Censure" enact the self's coming to terms with the influence of others as well as the experience of its own intellectual, emotional, and spiritual awakenings and failures. The volume's central figure of the open house stands as an early constituting metaphor for Roethke's confessional aesthetic: "My secrets cry aloud," he writes, "I have no need for tongue. / My heart keeps open house, / My doors are widely swung."[5]

In "The Lost Son"—Roethke's long poem that inaugurates his thematic explorations into depth psychology—the "open house" becomes the "empty house" of psychic ennui and melancholia. The metaphor of the open house changes in *The Lost Son* volume to the figure of the greenhouse as the dominant symbol of the self's interior, existential world. Roethke has called the hothouse a "symbol for the whole of life, a womb, a heaven-on-earth" (PC, 39). The glasshouses, he said, were "both heaven and hell, a kind of tropics created in the savage climate of Michigan. . . . It was a universe, several worlds, which, even as a child, one worried about, and struggled to keep alive . . ." (PC, 8–9). The poet's recollection of that childhood world, as Kenneth Burke has pointed out, serves as a scenic counterpart to Roethke's own imaginative growth.[6] The forcing-house setting also stages Roethke's need as the lost son to work through his psychic ambivalence toward the dead patriarch Otto Roethke, and by extension the fathering "great dead" of literary tradition.

The drama of gaining "the edge" on his poetic precursors compelled Roethke to conceive important innovations in lyric expression. His imaginative courage to "stand up to a great style"—to

OVERVIEW

venture "an influence survived" (PC, 68, 70)—empowers his strongest works with an intensity of imaginative vision few other poets possess. "He more than any other," James Dickey says, "is a poet of pure being."[7] In writing a poetry of pure being, Roethke pioneered new directions in poetic form, style, and themes. Unlike Eliot's Modernist poetry of abstract meditation and dense cultural allusion, Roethke achieves more direct and penetrating insights into nature, regional locales, the subtle life of things, embodied experience, and intuitive rather than analytic modes of understanding the world. "There is no poetry anywhere," Dickey asserts, "that is so valuably conscious of the human body as Roethke's; no poetry that can place the body in an *environment*—wind, seascape, greenhouse, forest, desert, mountainside, among animals, or insects, or stones . . ." (220). Roethke's central settings and subjects are akin to the kind of Romantic nostalgia for pastoral experience reminiscent of the "low and rustic" life celebrated by William Wordsworth. Moreover, like Whitman, Roethke held a special reverence for the regional locales of American place.

Typically, nature's organic wilderness serves as the scenic precondition for self-knowledge and spiritual illumination in his mature lyric verse. Having grown up in rural Saginaw, Roethke had a remarkable knowledge of plant and animal life, whose rich variety he records with the eye of an expert in his poetry's long catalogues of flora and fauna. Roethke's poetic virtuosity in depicting nature begins at one extreme with the seedlings' small sprouts that he carefully observes in the greenhouse sequence. But his verse ranges all the way to the large seasonal rhythms presented, for example, in the spring thaw of the ice-bound Tittebawasee river in "North American Sequence": "As the piled ice breaks away from the battered spiles, / And the whole river begins to move forward, its bridges shaking" (CP, 191).

Through such careful attention to the physical world—with "the eye close on the object" (PC, 83)—Roethke aimed for direct participation in natural process. As early as 1950 in "Open Letter" and three years later in "An American Poet Introduces Himself and His Poems," Roethke stressed the importance of place as the "means of establishing personal identity" (PC, 19). Saginaw's setting and, in particular, his family's greenhouse world, provided the poet with a constituting metaphor through which to define the self. His poetic sympathy for the subtle presences disclosed in this immediate, physical environment gave him alternative experiential, intuitive, and finally sacred modes of insight beyond rational, analytic, and scientific knowledge.

Roethke's poetic sympathy for the subhuman—his imaginative fusion with nature and the unconscious—ultimately opens onto what Nathan A. Scott, Jr. has described as a poetics of the sacred.[8] But Roethke's theology—his attempt to understand "The nature of God Himself" (PC, 19)—is neither grounded in Christian orthodoxy as is Eliot's, nor shaped by a private mythic system as is Blake's or Yeats's. Nevertheless, he is a poet of profound spirituality. To begin with, Roethke's visionary mysticism emerges, paradoxically, from the poet's regressive identification with nature's primitive and subhuman forms. "Sometimes, of course, there is regression. I believe that the spiritual man must go back in order to go forward" (PC, 12). This regressive aesthetic resembles, in some ways, Whitman's presentation of the self's progress as both a centripetal descent into the organic particulars of nature and a centrifugal expansion into the cosmos. "It is paradoxical," Roethke said, "that a very sharp sense of the being, the identity of some other being—and in some instances, even an inanimate thing—brings a corresponding heightening and awareness of one's own self and even more mysteriously, in some instances, a feeling of the oneness of the universe" (PC, 25).

Ultimately, what Roethke wanted was to fuse the secular and the sacred—to join perception and intellect, sensation and thought, the life of the body and the life of the mind. He aimed to retrieve the kind of unified experience he read in Elizabethan and Metaphysical verse, before what Eliot described as Modernism's "dissociation of sensibility" or the severing of emotions, the senses, and ideas from one another.[9] Quoting from his own metaphysical lyric "The Waking," Roethke wrote in his essay "On 'Identity'": " 'We think by feeling. What is there to know?' This, in its essence is a description of the metaphysical poet who thinks with his body: an idea for him can be as real as the smell of a flower or a blow on the head" (PC, 27). Like the Romantic and Metaphysical poets he admired, Roethke struggled to be "delivered from the rational into the realm of pure song" (CP, 172).

In pursuit of a "unified sensibility," the poet often finds himself "At the edge of the field waiting for the pure moment" (CP, 168) of fusion with nature. In terms of his poetry's imagery such moments, where person and place interpenetrate, are often presented in scenes of ecstatic illumination as in "I Waited": "The sun burned through a haze, / And I became all that I looked upon. / I

dazzled in the dazzle of a stone" (CP, 247). Moreover, the particular images of Roethke's poetic
landscapes often assume symbolic depth as Denis
Donoghue has noticed: "The life-enhancing images are rain, rivers, flowers, seed, grain, birds,
fish, veins. The danger signals are wind, storm,
darkness, drought, shadow. And the great event is
growth, in full light."[10] Not just a nature poet,
Roethke presents figurative models for the self's
spiritual development.

Beyond the particular images of Roethke's
nature poetry, his major constituting metaphor for
the progress of the self—"from I to Otherwise"
(PC, 25)—is the spiritual journey. The fourteen
long sequence poems of the poet's middle career—
comprising section 4 of *The Lost Son*, plus nine long
poems from *Praise to the End!* and "O, Thou Opening, O" from *The Waking*—Roethke described as
constituting a "history of the psyche (or allegorical
journey)" (PC, 39). Each of these middle works, he
wrote, "is a stage in a kind of struggle. . . to
become something more" (PC, 37). These major
stages, as the poet himself defined them, are not
wholly discrete but "repeat themselves, thrust
themselves upon us, again and again, with variation and change" (PC, 39).

The *Praise to the End!* sequence builds on
Roethke's "prenatal" greenhouse poems that de-

pict nature's tiny beginnings, as in "Cuttings (later)." Moving beyond the organic microcosm of the greenhouse poems, Roethke's project is to present a kind of psychic history of the self's formative years from birth through adolescence. In conveying his complex vision of the multiplicity of modern experience, Roethke expands these short lyrics into long extended meditations on the self's relationship to others, nature, time, death, the unconscious, and so on. "We must permit poetry," he wrote, "to extend consciousness as far, as deeply, as particularly as it can . . ." (PC, 83). Highly experimental and often disorienting, the *Praise to the End!* poems, in particular, are apt to give readers the most difficulty as they are written in an associative, surrealistic style—"psychic shorthand" as Roethke described it (PC, 42).

The opening poems of the *Praise to the End!* sequence present the irrational and spontaneous musings of the infant's world largely through nonsense lyrics and Mother Goose rhymes. Roethke described "Where Knock Is Open Wide" as "written entirely from the viewpoint of a very small child: all interior drama; no comment; no interpretation" (PC, 41). "I Need, I Need," likewise, the poet wrote, "opens with very oral imagery, the child's world of sucking and licking" (PC, 10). The remaining pieces chart the self's journey out of

OVERVIEW

nature through the awakening to adolescent sexuality in "Give Way, Ye Gates" and erotic joy in "Praise to the End!" "The Lost Son" was originally published as the title piece of Roethke's second volume together with "The Long Alley," "A Field of Light," and "The Shape of the Fire." Later these poems were assembled as central works in the *Praise to the End!* sequence.

"The Lost Son" can be considered generally as a poem of initiation—one that enacts the self's rite of passage into adulthood and spiritual awakening. Based on his first manic incident in 1935, the five sections of "The Lost Son" begin with the poet's regressive flight into the subhuman world of toads, snails, birds, and other creatures. The poem's middle sections—"The Pit" and "The Gibber"—descend toward the "deep" psychic landscapes of the personal unconscious. Here the poet is reconciled to the dead patriarch Otto Roethke in section 4 "The Return" and the luminous section 5 "It was beginning winter." In these last two movements, Roethke communes with the "lively understandable spirit" of "stillness" and light" (CP, 58). Several of the later pieces in the *Praise to the End!* sequence such as "Unfold! Unfold!" "I Cry, Love! Love!," and "O Thou Opening, O" complete the spirit's communion with what the poet describes as "A house for wisdom; a field for revelation. / . . . where light is" (CP, 90).

Beyond the constituting metaphor of the self's spiritual journey, Roethke celebrates the Divine in closed-form love poems published mainly after his marriage to Beatrice O'Connell in 1953. These often formalist pieces were inspired by love lyrics of sixteenth-and seventeenth-century English literature. In addition to *The Waking*'s memorable sequence "Four for Sir John Davies," Roethke published sixteen love lyrics in the "Love Poems" section of *Words for the Wind* and thirteen more in section 2 of his posthumous volume *The Far Field*. Moreover, several of the works from "Mixed Sequence" and "Sequence, Sometimes Metaphysical" of *The Far Field* take love as their central theme. In "The Dance" and "The Partner"—works that emerged through the poet's study of Sir John Davies, Sir Walter Raleigh, and W. B. Yeats—Roethke joins the imagery of earthly to divine love through the figure of the dance of secular with sacred experience. Here the poet explores the senses and significance of physical desire, affirming that "The body and the soul know how to play / In that dark world where gods have lost their way" (CP, 106). Later works, such as "Words for the Wind," "I Knew a Woman," "She," "The Other," and "The Sententious Man," join body

OVERVIEW

and soul as dancing "partners," often asserting erotic experience as an access to the Divine.

Several of these mature works depict the "dance" of soul and body as only one moment in the general reconciliation of seeming opposites: spirituality/sensuality, the sacred/the profane, love/lust, intellect/instinct, light/darkness, ecstasy/torpor, euphoria/despair, and life/death. Roethke's later metaphysical lyrics also probe this kind of contrary wisdom whose paradoxes defy rational logic. In the refrain to his famous villanelle, "The Waking," for example, Roethke asserts that "I wake to sleep, and take my waking slow. . . . / I learn by going where I have to go" (CP, 108). Similarly, his late formalist lyric "In a Dark Time" comprises such contradictory statements as, "In a dark time, the eye begins to see" or "Dark, dark my light, and darker my desire." Such ambiguities bespeak the poet's altered states of consciousness where "The mind enters itself, and God the mind, / And one is One, free in the tearing wind" (CP, 239). As several of Roethke's critics have shown in readings of "Mixed Sequence" and "Sequence, Sometimes Metaphysical," the poet derived his paradoxical understanding of mystical experience, in part, from his reading of Evelyn Underhill's comprehensive book *Mysticism: A study in the nature and development of Man's spiritual consciousness* (1955).

In particular, Roethke was impressed with Underhill's five-stage process of the self's mystical encounters with the Divine: (1) Awakening, (2) Purgation of the self, (3) Illumination or a sense of the divine order, (4) Dark night of the Soul, (5) Singleness, or the "discovery of God in oneself." These stages, it should be noted, serve as counterparts to one another. According to Underhill, the process of achieving mystical vision is characterized by moments of ecstatic oneness versus those of traumatic self-purgation. Roethke's late canon can be viewed as a kind of spiritual record of just how far he pursued these encounters with the "pure moment" of mystical ecstasy. While some poems celebrate individual stages of Underhill's five-part scheme—for example, the descent into the dark night of the soul of "In Evening Air" versus the celebration of the One in "Once More, The Round"—Roethke's strongest metaphysical lyrics, such as "The Abyss" and "In a Dark Time," incorporate the entire range of mystical understanding.

The distinctive subjects, themes, imagery, symbolism, and attitudes toward experience that unify the evolving Roethke canon culminate in his late magnum opus "North American Sequence." Roethke's American long poem rivals those of Eliot and Whitman, even as it builds on his precursors'

OVERVIEW

own characteristic motives and verbal styles. As the title implies, these long posthumously published pieces bespeak the poet's profound devotion to the American landscape, moving westward from Saginaw through the midwest landscapes of his youth, into the Dakotas and the Tetons, on to Puget Sound, and finally the North American coastline. Roethke's close attention to the delicate textures and subtle gestures discovered in America's plant and animal kingdoms follows his long-standing conviction that "Out of these nothings / —All beginnings come" (CP, 188). Consistently throughout his career, he stove to extend these beginnings as far as they would possibly lead— even to the "imperishable quiet at the heart of form" (CP, 188). In such "pure moments," the poet becomes "the end of all things, the final man"; that is, he encompasses American place within "the pure serene of memory in one man" (CP, 201).

The long poems of the "Sequence" taken together constitute what the poet describes as "the long journey out of the self" (CP, 193) in "Journey to the Interior." They thus stand as an outward, centrifugal counterpart to the centripetal greenhouse musings of *The Lost Son*. Moreover, they complete the long allegory of spiritual journeying throughout the whole of the *Praise to the End!*

sequence. In addition, the expansive movement of Roethke's final man—going beyond the enclosures of the greenhouse microcosm and toward the organic macrocosm of the American landscape—complements the glasshouse reveries of "Meditations of an Old Woman," the final long poem of *Words for the Wind*.

The poet's meditations on place in the six long poems that make up "North American Sequence" alternate between the scenic locales of earth and water, shore and surf. "The Longing" begins inland in the Dakotas' "country of few lakes" (CP, 189). In "Meditation at Oyster River" Roethke contrasts the serene, meditative rhythm of the tide-ripples—presumably of Puget Sound—with a memorable passage dramatizing the violent thaw of the Tittebawasee River. Similarly, the rugged western landscape of canyons and arroyos of "Journey to the Interior" presents a scenic contrast to the northwest coastline "where the fresh and salt waters meet" (CP, 196) in "The Long Waters." "The Far Field," like "Journey," begins "at the field's end" moving seaward through the river imagery of section 3 and a celebration in section 4 of the "sea-shapes" the "lost self" assumes in becoming the final man.

In "The Rose," the final poem of "North American Sequence," Roethke employs a traditional icon of eternal oneness—as in Yeats's "To the Rose Upon the Rood of Time"—in order to evoke the unity of person and place. The rose not only blooms out of the spatial intersection of shore and surf, it is also a figure for temporal continuity, "Flowering out of the dark, / Widening at high noon . . ." (CP, 203). Moreover, the rose too is a symbol for ecstatic, mystical vision—teaching the poet to assume the simple grace of "The single one," "Beyond becoming and perishing, / A something wholly other" (CP, 205). "The Rose" completes the poet's journey out of the self to which the hybrids beckoned him in his glasshouse recollections.

As a teaching poet, Roethke daily went about the business of helping students understand and appreciate the technical and stylistic resources of verse composition. Roethke's students—including such award-winning poets as Carolyn Kizer, David Wagoner, and James Wright—agree that he was an unusually dynamic and a genuinely engaging instructor. Through his teaching career, he developed a keen sense of poetry's performative dimension for an audience. In particular, he stressed the importance of "making the students aware of poetry as experience, making them hear it" (PC, 52). The poem's music or sound-sense was as important for Roethke as its visual imagery, subjects, and themes. Indeed, in the *Praise to the End!* poems he advises the reader to "*Listen* to them, for they are written to be heard" (PC, 37).

Roethke was convinced that certain sound and rhythmic patterns had the power to elicit unconscious responses in the reader, thus enacting the theme of regression. His characteristic diction relies heavily on onomatopoeia—the use of words to imitate and evoke actual sounds heard. Moreover, in his word choice, Germanic and Anglo-Saxon derivations predominate over Greek and Latin roots. Roethke used earthly, monosyllabic words "drenched with human association" in order to register experiential and psychic tones. "We all know," he claimed, "that poetry is shot through with appeals to the unconsciousness, to the fears and desires that go far back into our childhood, into the imagination of the race" (PC, 80).

One of the poet's aims in writing an evocative poetry was to evade the common sense, matter of fact rationality of adulthood in favor of the energy and wonder of childhood perception. Here poetry's sound and rhythms were crucial in the construction of childhood personae: "Rhythmically," he said, "it's the spring and rush of the child I am after" (PC, 41). Poetic language, Roethke thought, is inherently rhythmical as it draws from the organic pulse of life itself: "We must keep in

OVERVIEW

Kunitz's term for nature's metamorphic "protagonists" that people Roethke's verse: "Snail, snail, glister me forward, / Bird, soft-sigh me home, / Worm, be with me. / This is my hard time" (CP, 53). In the long developmental poems of his *Praise to the End!* sequence, as well as in the formal lyrics, Roethke employed the irrational, associative leaps of surrealistic imagination to "telescope image and symbol . . . without relying on the obvious connectives" (PC, 42). In fashioning an intuitive, emotive poetics, the strong poet, Roethke felt, "must create an actuality" (PC, 42). Other patterns that he utilized include the sharp repeated juxtapositions of image and striking maxim as in "The Shape of the Fire."

Roethke's unique style freely improvised with these and other techniques to present his visionary imagination as "dramatic revelation" (PC, 42). As Roethke's critics have discussed, such verbal performances provided important precedents and influential examples for a later generation of contemporary American writers. Critics now take for granted the explorations of depth psychology in the so-called deep-image writers, but as Anthony Libby has observed, Roethke was among the first to utilize the unconscious as a resource for postwar American poetry.[11] For all their significant differences, poets such as Robert Bly, James

Dickey, W. S. Merwin, and James Wright all learned much from Roethke's surrealistic descents into the psyche, the natural world, and the subhuman life of things. Moreover, the substantial risks Roethke undertook both personally and professionally by inaugurating a confessional poetics in the 1940s were crucial for a later generation of both male and female writers. Roethke's assertion of personal experience guided the writings of such poets as W. D. Snodgrass, Sylvia Plath, and Anne Sexton. Sexton recalled a telling observation she had made after reading *Colossus* a year before Plath's death and Roethke's in 1963: "saying something like . . . 'if you're not careful, Sylvia, you will out-Roethke Roethke', and she replied that I had guessed accurately and that he had been a strong influence on her work."[12]

Finally, Roethke's reclamation of regional landscapes as important subjects for American poetry had a direct bearing on poets as diverse as the "projectivist" writers (Charles Olson, Robert Duncan, and Denise Levertov), Northwest poets (Richard Hugo, Carolyn Kizer, William Stafford, and David Wagoner), Beat authors (Allen Ginsberg, Gary Snyder, and Phillip Whalen), and others such as A. R. Ammons, Galway Kinnell, and Mary Oliver. A pioneering writer of notable

OVERVIEW

imaginative courage, the Roethke abides as an influential figure for our foremost contemporary American poets.

Notes

1. Allan Seager, *The Glass House: The Life of Theodore Roethke* (New York: McGraw-Hill, 1968) 101.

2. Charles Molesworth *The Fierce Embrace* (Columbia, MO: University of Missouri Press, 1979) 23.

3. See Karl Malkoff, *Theodore Roethke: An Introduction to the Poetry* (New York: Columbia University Press, 1966).

4. Theodore Roethke, "How to Write Like Somebody Else," in *On the Poet and His Craft, Selected Prose of Theodore Roethke*, ed. Ralph J. Mills, Jr. (Seattle, WA: University of Washington Press, 1965) 70 (hereafter cited in the text as PC).

5. Theodore Roethke, *The Collected Poems of Theodore Roethke* (Seattle, WA: University of Washington Press, 1982) 3 (hereafter cited in the text as CP). The 1982 University of Washington Press volume is an offset reprint of the Doubleday 1966 *Collected Poetry*, assembled by Beatrice Roethke, Stanley Kunitz, and Frank Jones, and widely regarded as the definitive version of the Roethke canon. The pagination and contents of the University of Washington Press text match that of the Doubleday text with the single exception of the poem "Frau Bauman, Frau Schmidt, and Frau Schwartze," reintroduced at the end of the greenhouse poems in subsequent reprints of the Doubleday edition. The Doubleday/Anchor paperback reprint (1975) differs slightly in pagination but otherwise conforms to the 1982 text. While each of these volumes has the same claim to textual authority. I have chosen to quote from the 1982 reprint as it both includes the missing greenhouse poem and retains the same pagination of the original 1966 edition. See Stiffler (46–48) for a detailed critical discussion of the textual history of "Frau Bauman."

6. See Kenneth Burke, "The Vegetal Radicalism of Theodore Roethke," *Sewanee Review* 58 (Winter 1950) 68–108.

7. James Dickey, "The Greatest American Poet," in *Sorties: Journals and New Essays* (Garden City, NY: Doubleday, 1971) 220.

8. See Nathan A. Scott, Jr., "The Example of Roethke," in *The Wild Prayer of Longing: Poetry and the Sacred* (New Haven, CT: Yale University Press, 1971) 76–118.

9. See T. S. Eliot, "The Metaphysical Poets," in *Selected Essays* (New York: Harcourt Brace, 1960) 241–50.

10. Denis Donoghue, "Theodore Roethke's Broken Music," in *Theodore Roethke, Essays on the Poetry*, ed. Arnold Stein (Seattle, WA: University of Washington Press, 1965) 153.

11. Anthony Libby, "Roethke, Water Father," *American Literature* 46 (November 1974) 288.

12. Anne Sexton, "The Barfly Ought to Sing," in *The Art of Sylvia Plath*, ed. Charles Newman (Bloomington, IN: Indiana University Press, 1970) 178.

CHAPTER TWO

Open House

Ten years went into the writing of Roethke's first volume *Open House* (1941). During the last three years of concentrated editing from 1936–39, he consulted with Pulitzer Prize winner and long-time friend Stanley Kunitz on the final drafts of individual poems and the general format of the whole book. Roethke, like Yeats and Eliot, was both a gifted and shrewd writer, putting many hours into cultivating an audience for the volume. As one index of the poet's early success, reviews in such important journals as the *New Yorker*, the *Saturday Review*, the *Kenyon Review*, and the *Atlantic* were unanimously enthusiastic. W. H. Auden called *Open House* "completely successful," while Louise Bogan welcomed Roethke as "a young poet with a real sense of lyric style."[1]

Despite the early critical applause that greeted this first work, Roethke himself later acknowledged it was largely derivative from other writers and only hints at the important stylistic innovations undertaken by the poet in subsequent volumes. "It took me ten years to complete one little book," he wrote, "and now some of the things in it seem to creak" (PC, 16). Part of what makes *Open House* a somewhat weaker version of Roethke's later poetry is the volume's dependence on the verse forms and poetic models of past authors. While teaching at Penn State University, Roethke read heavily in John Donne and William Blake; other influences that shaped his writing at this time included Leonie Adams, Louise Bogan, Emily Dickinson, Rolfe Humphries, Stanley Kunitz, and Elinor Wylie.

Roethke's reliance on these poetic mentors is plainly seen throughout the volume. Moreover, the whole book is dominated by the kind of formal craft and metaphysical irony then prized by American New Criticism. Roethke, of course, was very much aware of his poetic imitations throughout his career. Indeed, he not only admitted his sources in "On 'Identity' " in 1963, but earlier devoted another essay to the controversial issue of poetic influence in "How to Write Like Somebody Else" (1959). Not adverse to learning from past masters, he maintained that imitation "is one of the great methods, perhaps *the* method of learning to write" (PC, 69). Roethke even claimed in his journals that

OPEN HOUSE

"A poet is judged, in part, by the influences he resists."[2] Thus, literary tradition provided an important arena for testing the adequacy of his own stylistic experimentations. In teaching creative writing Roethke routinely assigned fixed forms to be used as models. But as a consequence, several of the poet's first virtuoso pieces, as his critics have detailed, border on poetic exercises in crafted imitation. For example, the influence of Emily Dickinson is clearly evident in "No Bird":

> Now here is peace for one who knew
> The secret heart of sound.
> The ear so delicate and true
> Is pressed to noiseless ground.
>
> Slow swings the breeze above her head,
> The grasses whitely stir;
> But in this forest of the dead
> No bird awakens her. (CP, 17)

Here Roethke employs Dickinson's characteristic common meter—quatrains of alternating iambic tetrameter and trimeter lines—as well as her rhyme scheme (*abab*) to present a thematic rumination on death which itself derives from the earlier writer's own meditations on mortality. Some of Roethke's poetic imitations as in "This Light Comes Brighter," as he admits, border on pastiche. The models Roethke follows here are Elinor Wylie and

Henry Vaughan. Wylie's poem itself derives from
Shelley, which further complicates Roethke's borrowings. Nevertheless, the poet drew an important lesson from this early exercise: "This example
illustrates, certainly, at least two things: a wrong
choice of diction; an unfortunate use of a
model. . . . the moral is don't imitate an imitator;
pastiche begets pastiche" (PC, 64).

Beyond these kinds of early discoveries, imitation served as a testing ground for measuring his
talent against powerful precursors. The poet's
struggle with notable mentors is a central theme
throughout the first volume. In "Feud," for instance, Roethke enacts his rivalry with past influences. The first and final stanzas frame Roethke's
poetic rivalry with the influence of his literary
ancestors. Here he learns to "dread / The menace
of ancestral eyes" (CP, 4). Other works, such as
"Auction" and "Sale," can be read as metaphoric
dramas of the poet's need to purge himself of the
excess baggage and antique forms of past writing.
Such clashes with tradition were part of an un-
avoidable rite of passage that Roethke described in
his essay "On 'Identity'." Poems such as "Feud"
are significant forerunners of longer meditations
on influence in "The Lost Son," for example, and
in other works throughout Roethke's later career.
Beyond Roethke's encounters with the challenges
and pitfalls of poetic imitation, *Open House* looks

forward to central concerns that are worked out in subsequent poems.

The volume's title piece, in particular, is an important poem that anticipates the unfolding drama of the self in quest of identity, a key theme that profoundly shapes the poet's entire career:

> My secrets cry aloud.
> I have no need for tongue.
> My heart keeps open house,
> My doors are widely swung.
> An epic of the eyes
> My love, with no disguise. (CP, 3)

Focusing on the self is a strategic choice that departs from modernist doctrines of impersonality articulated, for example, in T. S. Eliot's landmark essay "Tradition and the Individual Talent": "The progress of an artist," Eliot maintained, "is a continual self-sacrifice, a continual extinction of personality."[3] Unlike Eliot, Roethke featured the confessional program of sharing the self's most intimate and unsettling moments with the reader. By grounding poetic subjects in direct "naked" personal experience, his project opposed American New Criticism's strictures against what W. K. Wimsatt and Monroe Beardsley later described as the intentional fallacy.[4] Nevertheless, Roethke's tightly organized closed-form lyrics, composed, as he says here, "In language strict and pure," satisfied New Criticism's criterion of formal craft in the 1940s.

Of the confessional works of the first book, "The Premonition," "On the Road to Woodlawn," and "The Reminder" testify to Roethke's need to reconcile himself to the childhood loss of his father, the subject of "The Lost Son." There is also the drama here of the self's certain truths that contradict and struggle against worldly ignorance. Works such as "Long Live the Weeds," "Against Disaster," and "Reply to Censure" assert a "dignity within, / And quiet at the core" against the "pedantry" of the "Defamers of the good," who "mock the deepest thought" (CP, 20). The poet's need to purge himself of imperfection, especially of the bodily kind, is an early theme taken up in *Open House*. Works such as "Epidermal Macabre" find the poet mired in "the savage blood's obscenity" and the flesh's mortal "cloak of evil and despair" (CP, 19). "Prayer" employs a metaphysical conceit of purging the body's fallen senses of taste, smell, touch, and hearing in favor of the eye's more spiritual insight. Reflecting back on this early concern in a 1955 biographical essay, Roethke said, "I have tried to transmute and purify my 'life', the sense of being defiled by it, in both small and formal and somewhat blunt short poems" (PC, 15).

More revealing, however, are the book's confessional moments where the self is invaded and

overwhelmed by the confusion of adult experience—the kind of doubts, uncertainties, and
moods of manic-depression that Roethke experienced first in 1935 and that recurred periodically
thereafter for the rest of his life. "Silence," for
example, depicts "the spirit crying in a cage"
amidst "Confusion's core set deep within / A
furious, dissembling din" (CP, 22), while "Prayer
Before Study" finds the poet "constricted" by
"tortured thought" (CP, 24). Other works are more
directly autobiographical in dramatizing the poet's
anxiety that his mental disturbances might stem
from a family inheritance. "My Dim-Wit Cousin"
climaxes in Roethke's arresting identification with
an unbalanced relative: "Your palm is moist, your
manner far too jolly. . . / Today while scraping hair
before the mirror, / My shaving hand jerked back
in sudden terror: / I heard your laughter rumble
from my belly" (CP, 25). Even in these first works
Roethke could view his periodic mood swings
critically, eventually exploiting them as a resource
for his poetic art.

However one diagnoses his manic-depressive
incidents, Roethke experienced them as profoundly mystical events. His mental breakdown of
1935, as Neal Bowers has shown, was for the poet
an intense spiritual initiation, one that led Roethke
to incorporate the intuitive and irrational both
thematically and stylistically into his verse.[5] "I like

to think a thing part way through," he said, "and feel the rest of the way" (SF, 152). Several poems in *Open House* dwell on Roethke's lifelong interest in mystical experience that exceeds conventional rationality. The tension between feeling and thought, intuition and rational analysis, is the subject of "The Signals" and "Genesis" that praise moments of instinctual understanding where "Sometimes the blood is privileged to guess / The things the eye or hand cannot possess" (CP, 8).

Roethke's spiritual journey out of the self led him into a profound sympathy for nature and the plant and animal lives of regional America. The poet's mystical participation in nature can be read as a metaphor for his theory of poetry's organic form. Jay Parini situates Roethke's organic imagination in the Romantic tradition of Wordsworth, Coleridge, Emerson, and Whitman. "The great Romantic model for the creative process, which flows and does not freeze, is the botanical organism."[6] The poet's Romantic nostalgia for nature and regional landscapes shape "The Light," "Slow Season," "Mid-Country Blow," "In Praise of Prairie," "The Coming of the Cold," and "Night Journey," looking forward to the celebrated greenhouse poems of *The Lost Son and Other Poems*, as well as the characteristic locales of American place, Midwest and Northwest, in subsequent volumes. Moreover, Roethke's visionary elevation of nature as an access to God further joins him to the transcendentalism of Emerson and Whitman: "The idea of salvation underlies this poetics, and Roethke writes directly in this tradition; his poetry is secular religion or, in Carlyle's phrase, natural supernaturalism."[7] Yet Roethke's "secular religion" often leads to insights that are not so much beautific as demonic. "The Heron" and "The Bat" pay close attention to nature for metaphoric emblems of the self. The benign antics of the bat, for instance, at first seem harmless enough as "He loops in crazy figures half the night" (CPE, 16). In a closer encounter it embodies a more unsettling natural mystery that recalls Eliot's horrific image of "bats with baby faces in the violet light"[8] from *The Waste Land*:

> But when he brushes up against a screen,
> We are afraid of what our eyes have seen:
> For something is amiss or out of place
> When mice with wings can wear a human face.
> (CPE, 16)

The estrangement of the bat's regard fuses the human with the subhuman, a theme Roethke enacts continually throughout his career.

Open House, then, can be considered as a harbinger of Roethke's mature poetry. However carefully crafted, it relies too heavily on poetic imitation. Although this first volume is not stylistically representative of the poet's subsequent career, it serves nevertheless as a key index to central themes developed throughout the Roethke canon. A close reading of these first poems provides a useful introduction to Roethke's major concerns: the poet's struggle with literary precursors, his confessional focus, his reliance on nature and pastoral subjects, and finally his motif of the spiritual journey out of the self.

Notes

1. Allan Seager, *The Glass House* 127.

2. Theodore Roethke, *Straw for the Fire: From the Notebooks of Theodore Roethke*, ed. David Wagoner (Garden City, NY: Doubleday, 1972) 176 (hereafter cited in the text as SF).

3. T. S. Eliot, "Tradition and the Individual Talent," in *Selected Essays* 7.

4. See William K. Wimsatt and Monroe C. Beardsley "The Intentional Fallacy," in *The Verbal Icon: Studies in the Meaning of Poetry* (Lexington, KY: University of Kentucky Press, 1954) 3–18.

5. See Neal Bowers, *Theodore Roethke: The Journey from I to Otherwise* (Columbia, MO: University of Missouri Press, 1982).

6. Jay Parini, *Theodore Roethke: An American Romantic* (Amherst, MA: University of Massachusetts Press, 1979) 35.

7. Parini 37.

8. T. S. Eliot, *The Complete Poems and Plays, 1909–1950* (New York: Harcourt Brace, 1971) 48 (hereafter cited in the text as CPE).

CHAPTER THREE

The Lost Son and Other Poems

Roethke published *The Lost Son* in 1948, seven years after *Open House,* and as Stanley Kunitz has said, it was "the confirmation that he was in full possession of his art and of his vision."[1] Roethke readers have been unanimous in their praise for *The Lost Son,* but several critics view it as the early climax of his poetic talent. In his essay "A Green House Eden" Louis Martz claims that "Roethke never surpassed the achievement of *The Lost Son.*"[2] Others, however, view it more as the foundation for Roethke's later writing. William Meredith argues for a steady increase in Roethke's powers, comparing *The Lost Son* to Yeats's *A Vision* in providing a mythic source for the unfolding of Roethke's more mature work.[3]

The opening fourteen poems of *The Lost Son,* the greenhouse poems, inaugurate Roethke's concern for nature's obscure microcosm of organic growth. Here he makes contact with the "pure, sensuous form" (CP, 150) of natural process. Within this subterranean scene, the poet encounters the local energies, rhythms, and textures that together manifest a primal life-urge. The poet's verbal techniques in these poems reflect this kind of primal witnessing. Roethke prunes away any authorial distance, blocking his attention to nature's flux. His art reflects a vital immediacy disclosed in the hidden world of bulbs, shoots, and cuttings. That organic struggle, Roethke said, should be "rendered dramatically, without comment, without allusion, the action often implied or indicated in the interior monologue" (PC, 10).

Roethke's stylistic use of hyphenation, irregular strong-stress rhythms, and colloquial diction create primitive effects in the opening poem, "Cuttings." Here the poet presents a kind of time-lapse view of root systems drawing nourishment from the micro-environment of "sand-crumbs" (CP, 137). Roethke's use of intransitive verbs ("droop," "dries," "bulge") and his eye for striking detail ("pale tendrilous horn") invest the natural processes of cellular growth with a unique strangeness.

In "Some Remarks on Rhythm" Roethke described how the use of Anglo-Saxon monosyllabic words can create an intuitive and evocative poetics. Such direct and rustic speaking, he said, appeals to our basic rooting in the unconscious. "We all know that poetry is shot through with appeals to the unconsciousness, to the fears and desires that go far back into our childhood, into the imagination of the race. And we know that some words, like *hill, plow, mother, window, bird, fish,* are so drenched with human association, they sometimes can make even bad poems evocative" (PC, 80). Moreover, by hyphenating nouns and modifiers into unexpected surrealistic juxtapositions ("sticks-in-a-drowse," "slug-soft," "thorn-bitten," "snuff-laden," "stem-fur," "monkey-tails," "adder-mouthed"), Roethke jars one's conventional experience of nature. By employing assonance, consonance, onomatopoeia, and spondaic stress patterns, he recreates the alien textures of the glasshouse landscape. Another technique used to evoke nature's irrational rhythms is the disruption of the iambic line with strong stress and sprung rhythms. In two essays, "How to Write Like Somebody Else" and "Some Remarks on Rhythm," Roethke explained how irregular stress patterns can achieve "memorable" and "passionate" verbal performances: "If we concern ourselves with more primitive effects in poetry, we come inevitably to consideration, I think, of verse that is closer to prose. And here we jump rhythmically to a kind of opposite extreme. For many strong stresses, or playing against an iambic pattern to a loosening up, a longer, more irregular foot, I agree that free verse is a denial in terms" (PC, 81). Roethke's goal in such experiments with language and prosody is to invoke and mime the spontaneous, organic life he finds in nature. But his close attention to the garden world serves a further end. The small yet exemplary "beginnings" he witnesses in the greenhouse nurseries, as Kenneth Burke pointed out, are metaphoric models for Roethke's own imaginative growth toward a mature self.[4]

This correspondence between self and landscape is the explicit subject of "Cuttings (later)." Roethke's tentative experiments with language flower out of the same "urge, wrestle, resurrection" (CP, 37) that the cuttings undergo. Stanza 2 shifts this close observation of nature inward as Roethke interiorizes his witnessing of outer growth:

> I can hear, underground, that sucking and sob-
> bing,
> In my veins, in my bones I feel it,—
> The small water seeping upward,
> The tight grains parting at last.
> When sprouts break out,
> Slippery as fish,
> I quail, lean to beginnings, sheath-wet. (CP, 37)

So intense is the poet's sympathy for this sprouting

THE LOST SON AND OTHER POEMS

that he hears "underground" the visceral "urge, wrestle, resurrection" of "new life." Poetry in these writings is Roethke's way of consecrating the "sheath wet" beginnings of vegetal birth in the greenhouse.

The "Cuttings" group enacts a primal, organic struggle that sparks correspondent beginnings within the poet's interior life. To behold the self's organic underpinnings is also, for Roethke, to suffer one's own imaginative birth. Typically the poet's awakening to nature happens only through a traumatic loss of his "normal," subjective identity. In "River Incident," from section 3 of *The Lost Son,* Roethke's alien contact with the water's small lives suddenly dissolves all the cultural fictions that divide the self from nature:

> A shell arched under my toes,
> Stirred up a whirl of silt
> That riffled around my knees.
> Whatever I owed to time
> Slowed in my human form. (CP, 49)

"River Incident" 's unnerving moment of déjà-vu washes away centuries of human evolution, baptizing the poet into the knowledge of the "cold, granitic slime" of primal "sea water." Roethke enters into communion with the subhuman only through such primal self-effacements. The sudden erosion of identity is the precondition for achieving oneness with nature.

Such estranged revelations typify the poet's regressive participation in the primitive. This organic poetics, based in the immediate reality of local place, emerges from his even more fundamental aesthetic principle of regression: "Sometimes, of course there is regression. I believe that the spiritual man must go back in order to go forward" (PC, 12). "Going back" meant many things for Roethke. In this volume it entails a return to the recollected landscapes of his youth—Michigan's Saginaw valley. In his essay "Open Letter" Roethke discussed how the Michigan landscape provided him a distinctively American source of inspiration: "Some of these pieces, then, begin in the mire; as if man is no more than a shape writhing from the old rock. This may be due, in part, to the Michigan from which I come. Sometimes one gets the feeling that not even the animals have been there before; but the marsh, the mire, the Void, is always there, immediate and terrifying. It is a splendid place for schooling the spirit. It is America" (PC, 40). "The marsh, the mire, the Void" is a typically American locale because its forceful "otherness" resists the poet's attempts to master or exhaust its alien frontiers. The primordial reality of the local renders Roethke as "no more than a shape writhing" before nature's "immediate and terrifying" void.

Roethke's regressive aesthetic leads to a subterranean vision of organic struggle devoid of the ordering intelligence of aesthetic form. In "Root Cellar" the poet uncovers an amorphous underworld lorded over by bulbs and shoots with "long yellow evil necks, like tropical snakes" (CP, 38). The serpentine forms "piled against slippery planks" are fecund, but mindless. Roethke voices the garden world's often repulsive vitality through an evocative, onomatopoetic language:

> Scums, mildews, smuts along stems
> Great cannas or delicate cyclamen tips,—
> All pulse with the knocking pipes
> That drip and sweat,
> Sweat and drip,
> Swelling the roots with steam and stench,
> Shooting up lime and dung and ground bones.
> (CP, 38)

In "Forcing House" the throbbing rhythms of "Cuttings" return in Roethke's depiction of the life-urge of cannas and cyclamen. Roethke's rhythmic chiasmus imitates the prosaic cadence of the greenhouse's mindless pulse. Alliteration ("scums," "smuts," "stems," "cannas," "pulse," "sweat," "steam," "stench") recreates the hothouse atmosphere of hissing steam. These experiments with poetic language evoke a sense of what Frederick J. Hoffman calls the "prenatal condition" of the greenhouse nurseries.[5]

Beyond these primal beginnings, Roethke is also mindful of the local custodians who as primitive artists direct the garden world toward higher aesthetic forms. "Old Florist" and "Frau Bauman, Frau Schmidt, and Frau Schwartze" both celebrate the rural greenhouse workers. Roethke depicts these garden masters as natural magicians in their special powers of cultivating and enriching life with art:

> Quicker than birds, they dipped
> Up and sifted the dirt;
> They sprinkled and shook;
> They stood astride pipes,
> Their skirts billowing out wide into tents,
> Their hands twinkling with wet. (CP 44)

The garden world's prosaic tasks of dipping, sifting, sprinkling, and shaking the earth together assume a magical vocation. The practical "witches" of the greenhouses seem almost supernatural as they keep "creation at ease" by sewing up the air and trellising the sun. In his article "The Vegetal Radicalism of Theodore Roethke," Kenneth Burke points out that such rural occupations are a Romantic inheritance from Wordsworth.[6] Roethke's

THE LOST SON AND OTHER POEMS

"Old Florist" is the contemporary incarnation of Wordsworth's "low and rustic life":

Tamping and stamping dirt into pots,—
How he could flick and pick
Rotten leaves or yellowy petals,
. . . Or fan life into wilted sweet-peas with his hat,
Or stand all night watering roses, his feet blue in rub-
   ber boots. (CP, 42)

Like Wordsworth's leech gatherer from "Resolution and Independence," the "Old Florist" transcends the mundane rusticity of his occupation through an almost divine power "to keep creation at ease."

Similar to "Old Florist," Roethke's self-portrait describes the transformation of nature into art through an earthy struggle. The "Weed Puller" penetrates to the garden's vital center—a tangle of "black hairy roots," "lewd monkey-tails," "webs and weeds" (CP, 39). But such thankless encounters with nature's organic underworld transfigure life's raw energies into aesthetic blossomings:

Tugging all day at perverse life:
The indignity of it!—
With everything blooming above me,
Lilies, pale-pink cyclamen, roses,
Whole fields lovely and inviolate,—
Me down in that fetor of weeds,

Crawling on all fours,
Alive, in a slippery grave. (CP, 39)

Karl Malkoff emphasizes the procreative aspect of
the "Weed Puller," conveyed through the words
"fetor" and "slippery grave": "The slippery
grave," he says, "is of course, the womb; the 'fetor'
suggests 'foetus.' "[7] Louis Martz views the poem's
final word "grave" as a reminder of mortality,
thereby balancing Malkoff's focus on the life-sustaining chore of the "Weed-Puller."[8] Malkoff and
Martz provide significant readings that together
join the poet to the American tradition of Whitman
and Stevens, who both celebrate the interpenetra-
tion of life and death.

Preserving the garden's aesthetic life from
nature's chaotic flux is a practical vocation that
Roethke learns from the garden workers. The poet
is first made aware of the continual discipline of art
from them. His aesthetic commitment to shelter
the garden world from nature's violence culminates in "Big Wind." Here he presents the "savage
climate of Michigan" through the imagery of a sea
storm. In the poem's controlling metaphor, the
garden workers as sailors navigate their cargo of
roses through the "core and pith" of nature's
typhoon. As in the previous worker poems,
Roethke's prosaic chores of draining the manure

THE LOST SON AND OTHER POEMS

machine, watching the steam pressure gauge, stuffing broken windows with burlap, and so on together assume an almost supernatural vocation in "Big Wind." These simple tasks sustain the environment nurturing the living cargo in the glasshouse. Similar to Romantic works like "Resolution and Independence," "Big Wind" features rustic occupations as exemplary models of human endurance in the face of nature's flux.

Stylistically, "Big Wind" is patterned after a more Modern than Romantic poetic strategy. The energetic images rely on participial verbs to evoke nature's dynamic immediacy: "ploughing," "bucking," "flailing," "flinging," "veering," "wearing," "whistling," and "carrying" (CP, 41). In almost every line, Roethke employs consonance, assonance, and onomatopoeia to register the discordant tones of natural chaos. Roethke's verbal performance achieves its power through a balanced tension of sound and sense. For Roethke, the poet like the garden worker must match the destructive force of nature's big wind with an equally rigorous imaginative strength. The idea of the poet's energy as a power that combats nature's violence is a modern concept—one that Wallace Stevens theorized in his essay "The Noble Rider and the Sound of Words": "But as a wave is a force and not the water of which it is composed, which is never the same, so nobility is a force and not the manifestations of which it is composed. . . . It is a violence from within that protects us from a violence without. It is the imagination pressing back against the pressure of reality."[9] Similarly, in "Big Wind" Roethke must adapt his criteria for aesthetic "nobility" to the quick metamorphosis of Michigan's violent weather. The poem's verbal power must fathom the "core and pitch" of reality's "ugly storm" and thereby give voice to Saginaw's "calm morning." By constantly balancing the tension between life and art, the accomplished poet, like the garden technician, achieves a noble reconciliation between the two.

The garden world is Roethke's constituting metaphor for this aesthetic harmony between human dwelling and its natural "other"—Michigan's "savage climate." Moreover, it stands as a scenic equivalent for the mature poet's mediation of internal and external experience. In the greenhouse sequence the rural worker is the exemplary mediator between the greenhouse's interior closure and nature's open-ended plain. *The Lost Son*'s regressive recollections mainly focus on the inward microcosm of the garden world. In the greenhouse poems Roethke's link to the macroscopic landscape beyond the glass walls is his father Otto Roethke,

THE LOST SON AND OTHER POEMS

who shelters the delicate order of the forcing house. The dramatic subject of "The Lost Son," Roethke's title piece, is the shock of Otto's death, which shatters the security of the poet's childhood world. The loss of the father, however, initiates the poet's own imaginative birth. Specifically, Otto's death triggers Roethke's process of psychic individuation.

A profoundly cathartic work, "The Lost Son" takes up the poet's private conflict of devotion and rivalry that formed the basis of his filial anxiety. It stands as a kind of confession to his lifelong ambivalence toward Otto. Similarly, "My Papa's Waltz" presents a compressed version of Roethke's vacillation toward his father, registering playful but poignant tones in stanzas of iambic trimeter:

> The whiskey on your breath
> Could make a small boy dizzy;
> But I hung on like death:
> Such waltzing was not easy (CP, 45)

Roethke's comments on "The Lost Son" in "Open Letter" illuminate the poem's thematic center: "The revelation of the identity of the speaker may itself be a part of the drama; or, in some instances, in a dream sequence, his identity may merge with someone else's, or be deliberately blurred. This struggle for spiritual identity is, of course, one of the perpetual recurrences" (PC, 41). Applying Jungian and Freudian theory to the poet's "struggle for spiritual identity," Karl Malkoff has pointed out the connection between the structure of Roethke's "developmental poems" and his recurring incidents of depression and psychological regression. He explains Roethke's unconscious complex in "The Lost Son" through the death of the patriarch during the poet's adolescence. This early tragedy does not allow Roethke to work through the son's normal filial rivalry. Consequently, the poet's unconscious guilt ultimately leads to his mental collapse and confinement at Ann Arbor's Mercywood Hospital in 1935.

The autobiographical opening of "The Lost Son"—"At Woodlawn I heard the dead cry," (CP, 53)—returns to the cemetery where Otto lies buried. Here among the dead, the poet begins his regressive quest for filial reconciliation. At the entrance to Woodlawn's recollected landscape Roethke confronts the metaphoric signs of his shattered psychological condition. He endures the toads, brooding wells, and hostile leaves by a deeper regressive identification with nature's small and humble creatures, celebrated in the greenhouse sequence. The garden world's subhuman fauna serve as allies against the lost son's "hard time."

THE LOST SON AND OTHER POEMS

In stanza 2 regressive flight moves inward through a metaphorical shift from remembered place to the psyche's old wound:

> Fished in an old wound,
> The soft pond of repose;
> Nothing nibbled my line,
> Not even minnows came. (CP, 53)

Abandonment, lifelessness, monotony, and despair all characterize Roethke's melancholic moods in the absence of the imagination's redemptive presence. The symbol for the lost son's ennui is the "empty house" where the poet languishes, "Watching shadows crawl, / Scratching" (CP, 53). In such reductive moments, Roethke's prosaic language invokes a desolate landscape devoid of mind or meaning. This tedium, compounded by outward absence and inner disarray, follows European surrealism's traditional poetics of ennui. "Breton and the other surrealists," according to Mary Ann Caws, "although they try to regain the child's attitude of *presence* and immediacy, are constantly haunted by the sense of inner disunity and by the more obvious outer division between man and his surroundings."[10] As in earlier versions of surrealism, Roethke's manic moments lead to antithetical moods of boredom, torpor, ennui, and internal stagnation.

Abandoned by nature and everywhere confronted with the same absence and lack, Roethke next invokes poetry's redemptive *logos*:

> Voice, come out of the silence.
> Say something. . . .
> Tell me: Which is the way I take;
> Out of what door do I go,
> Where and to whom? (CP, 54)

But such questioning leads nowhere, merely returning the poet to the earlier void. Moreover, the quest for meaning through language is confused by the endless feedback of words echoing through the empty house. Instead of providing a solution to his hard time, the poem's nonsensical answers only further regression:

> Dark hollows said, lee to the wind,
> The moon said, back of an eel,
> . . . You will find no comfort here,
> In the kingdom of bang and blab. (CP, 54)

The poet's blab stems from Mother Goose rhymes and infantile nonsense verse:

> Is it soft like a mouse?
> Can it wrinkle its nose?
> Could it come in the house
> On the tips of its toes? (CP, 54)

The subject and meaning of these rhymes and riddles are purposefully ambiguous. The deliber-

THE LOST SON AND OTHER POEMS

ately senseless blab frustrates attempts to assign it any determinate meaning. Roethke's strategy is to duplicate for the reader his experience of bewilderment in the face of the language of the unconscious. What is equally significant is the poem's redundant form. The compulsive repetition of nonsensical rhymes is an index of the poet's repressed unconscious complex. In "The Flight" the poet retreats into the instinctual lives of nature's subhuman creatures. As in "River Incident" Roethke descends back through evolutionary chronology, identifying with the rat "Running lightly over spongy ground" (CP, 53). Like the eel he further regresses back to the "quick-water," the "wrinkling and rippling" element of the unconscious.

"The Pit" furthers Roethke's questioning of nature's small enigmatic beings, leading to the poet's descent into the primordial landscapes of the unconscious. Here Roethke undergoes a kind of death to the ego's social disguises that conceal his underlying complex of filial guilt. Engaging the unconscious in "The Gibber" leads to primal catharsis. That is, by enduring the drama of the ego's individuation, the poet experiences an interior resurrection—his identification with the father principle. The depiction of primal memory in "The Gibber" parallels Mircea Eliade's existential definition of revery. Memory, for Eliade, is not an inert mental archive. Instead, he defines recollection as an active experiential encounter, altering secular time with mythic moments of duration: "The function of memory is not to *conserve* the memory of the primordial myth, but to transport the patient to *where that event is in the process of accomplishment*."[11] Recalling the deep unconscious landscapes of memory, the poet experiences a kind of mythic transport to a primordial time. "The Gibber" fuses present with primal moments through déjà vu:

> At the wood's mouth,
> By the cave's door,
> I listened to something
> I had heard before. (CP, 55)

Along with the confluence of secular and mythic time, the poet experiences the dissolution of the ego's social disguises. Roethke employs cosmic images to invoke the expansive awakening to the individuated self as a visceral confrontation with the unconscious:

> Dogs of the groin
> Barked and howled,
> The sun was against me,
> The moon would not have me.
>
> The weeds whined,
> The snakes cried,
> The cows and briars
> Said to me: Die. (CP, 55)

THE LOST SON AND OTHER POEMS

Here the entire cosmos—from sun and moon down through cows, snakes, briars, and weeds— conspires against the poet's social mask in a kind of curse that thrusts him through death. Utterances of bewildered wonder in stanza 4 further drama- tize the descent into the unconscious: "I'm cold. I'm cold all over. Rub me in father and mother. / Fear was my father, Father Fear. / His look drained the stones" (CP, 56). Approaching the repressed core of his filial estrangement—personified in the figure of "Father Fear"—Roethke once again is overwhelmed by emotions of absence and aban- donment. The vacancy of the empty house returns now as the silent cave of ice, where the poet confronts his unconscious anxiety. Compounding this awe in the presence of Father Fear is the biblical echo of God's questioning of Job: "Hath the rain a father?" (CP, 56).

In the next stanza a "gliding shape," "poised on the stair," beckons the poet onward in his regressive quest. The ghost, another of Otto's poetic incarnations, retreats down a staircase, a traditional symbol of mystical association that Roethke will again employ late in his career in "The Abyss." Otto's elusive ghost serves a similar purpose to Jung's shadow archetype in the indi- viduation process. As an emanation of the uncon- scious, the shadow alerts the ego to its current psychic needs. The "possessive" fascination the shadow exerts over the ego draws it deeper into the unconscious where its repressed complex can be worked through on the self's collective level.

"The Gibber"'s central question of stanza 8, "Is this the storm's heart?" bespeaks Roethke's awe in the face of interior apocalypse, where even "the ground is unstilling itself":

Is this the storm's heart? The ground is unstilling it-
    self.
My veins are running nowhere. Do the bones cast out
    their fire?
Is the seed leaving the old bed? These buds are live as
    birds.
Where, where are the tears of the world?
Let the kisses resound, flat like a butcher's palm;
Let the gestures freeze; our doom is already decided.
All the windows are burning! What's left of my life?
I want the old rage, the lash of primordial milk!
Goodbye, goodbye, old stones, the time-order is
    going,
I have married my hands to perpetual agitation,
I run, I run to the whistle of money. (CP, 56)

At first glance, most of Roethke's readers will find these lines disorienting to say the least. Resembling an Elizabethan rant scene, this meditation dwells on various contrarieties: life and death, the conscious and the unconscious, past and future, confusion and insight, despair and ecstasy, and so forth. For both Roethke and Jung, the experience of individuation "always feels like the end of the world, as though everything had tumbled back into original chaos."[12] Roethke further dramatizes death's entropy in images of physical exhaustion: "My veins are running nowhere. Do the bones cast out their fire?" The body's mortality leads to hopeful images of transplanting and renewal: "Is the seed leaving the old bed? These buds are live as birds." Stylistically, such rhetorical questions and exclamatory utterances convey the poet's awed witnessing to the self's individuation.

"The Gibber" achieves its memorable effects, in part, through these kinds of oxymoronic juxtapositions. Heightening the unified perspective on life and death, Roethke couples images into antithetical pairs: "Let the kisses resound, flat like a butcher's palm." These paradoxical usages bespeak, among other things, the tension between the ego's limited vision and the more expansive knowledge of the collective self. Roethke's empty house ignites finally and as all its windows burn, he realizes, too late, his central self-betrayal: "I have married my hands to perpetual agitation / I run, I run to the whistle of money." The whistle of money had dominated Roethke's professional career as a publicity writer at Lafayette College from 1931–35. His mental collapse at Michigan State

College in 1935 marked a crucial turning point in his commitments. Driven by the perpetual agitation of American consumer culture, Roethke could not achieve a balanced grounding in nature and the unconscious. His fictive mask failed to endure the apocalyptic inferno of the betrayed self. Such purging by fire of the old self prepares for the poet's awakening to a new understanding of natural mystery. Completing the redemptive transplanting of stanza 8, the final lines of "The Gibber" cleanse the "false" ego with the inundating waters of the collective unconscious.

Roethke's baptism in the "dark swirl" of the unconscious leads to communion with the paternal presence of "The Return." Filial anxiety occasions Roethke's regressive journey in quest of the paternal principle, now exiled deep within the psyche. Only by descending into this interior landscape and there enduring the death of the ego's false persona does the poet work through his estrangement. The opening of "The Return" radically alters the tone and imagery of "The Gibber." The childhood familiarity of the greenhouse world dispels the unsettling purgatory of the betrayed self. The chaotic scene that Roethke witnessed in "The Gibber" is banished in favor of the glasshouse's protective security. Morning light illuminates that

THE LOST SON AND OTHER POEMS

dark swirl and rejuvenates the landscape with a splendid, cool air:

> Once I stayed all night.
> The light in the morning came slowly over the white
> Snow.
> There were many kinds of cool
> Air.
> Then came steam. (CP, 57).

Roethke's enjambment of the monosyllables "Snow," and "Air" following on his lines ending with "white" and "cool" registers an abstract tone that prepares for communion with the father principle. Enjambment, the running of one line into another without terminal punctuation, is a technique Roethke uses here for stylistic emphasis. The life-sustaining warmth of paternal presence—as the poet recalls it in the lines "Ordnung! Ordnung! Papa is coming!" (CP, 57)—reverses the images of absence and frigidity in "The Gibber":

> A fine haze moved off the leaves;
> Frost melted on far panes;
> The rose, the chrysanthemum turned toward the
>   light.
> Even the hushed forms, the bent yellowy weeds
> Moved in a slow up-sway. (CP, 57)

Clearing the landscape of anxiety and remorse prepares for the full deployment of light as paternal presence in section 5, "It was beginning winter." Tempered by the psychic purgation of "The Gibber," Roethke's imaginative vision in this final section passes beyond the glasshouse's sheltering architecture:

> It was beginning winter,
> The light moved slowly over the frozen field
> Over the dry seed-crowns,
> The beautiful surviving bones
> Swinging in the wind. (CP, 58)

Although frozen with oncoming winter, the dry meadow manifests an essential beauty in its endurance of nature's harsh weather. The austere radiance of the surviving plain provides a stark contrast to the proliferating vitality of the hothouse climate. The same splendid epiphany the poet experiences in "The Return" now freely traverses the expansive outer plain. The poem closes on the lost son having communed with the luminous grace of a "lively understandable spirit" (CP, 58).

Achieving a mature poetic identity for Roethke entailed working through a filial aggression toward his father. But "The Lost Son" is not only "about" Roethke's private complex; the poem's form enacts his wider, literary rivalry with the paternal figures of his poetic tradition. Integral to the poet's quest for identity is his broader struggle to be reconciled

THE LOST SON AND OTHER POEMS

to his literary fathers. It is well known that the Modernists had a profound influence in Roethke's creative life. He even acknowledged his indebtedness to his precursors, especially Yeats, in "How to Write Like Somebody Else." But Roethke preferred to think of these older poets less as dominant rivals than as encouraging and supportive mentors. Nevertheless, the anxiety he revealed toward the Moderns nearly amounted to an obsession. In one instance he testified to the supernatural visitation of Yeats's ghost after having completed his Yeatsian poem "The Dance." This kind of confession shows just how highly charged was the force of prior writing in Roethke's process of composition. Although he affirmed his identification with precursors, the poet arrived at that positive coexistence only through a stylistic and thematic antagonism to the Modernists in his early career. "The Lost Son," in particular, stands as the initial expression of his struggle to achieve poetic identity.

Thoughout his career Roethke openly discussed the tension between his respect for, and rivalry with, his poetic fathers: Eliot, Yeats, and to a lesser extent, Blake, Stevens, and Whitman. In his essay "On 'Identity' " Roethke outlined the literary influences that shaped his work; there he claimed that every author must come to a personal sense of voice out of the struggle with one's literal and spiritual ancestors. For some critics, most notably Harold Bloom, Roethke was indeed overwhelmed by the powerful example of his Modernist mentors.[13] Several critics, likewise, charge Roethke with having a derivative talent, largely dependent on the "supreme masters" he so often praises.[14] This critical dismissal oversimplifies and even misrepresents Roethke's valuable contribution to various schools and movements of American poetry in the postwar epoch.

Emphasizing Roethke's failure to displace the aesthetics of High Modernism ignores both the powerful transformations his work accomplished within that tradition and the influential directions he pioneered for a later generation of Postmodern poets. In fact, Roethke's confessional exposure of self marks a powerful departure from the impersonal and universal themes of Modernist and New Critical poets. Instead of basing his poetry's subjects on historical, or mythic paradigms, Roethke opts for a more directly autobiographical performance. Unlike Eliot's doctrine of poetic impersonality in "Tradition and the Individual Talent," Roethke features his private experience of filial guilt in "The Lost Son." Moreover, Roethke's surrealistic style parts company with the Modernists.

"The Lost Son" is primarily a work that at

THE LOST SON AND OTHER POEMS

once mimics and challenges the characteristic verbal styles of Eliot and Yeats. Several of the poet's critics have called attention to Roethke's dialogue with his Modernist mentors. Roethke's linguistic borrowings blend the abstract and impersonal rhetoric of High Modernism with the colloquial speaking of the local American idiom and the imagery of regional landscape. Roethke's strategy for handling the overshadowing influence of Modernist discourse is most visible in the rhetorical techniques of "The Gibber." There Roethke's primordial settings seem drained of traditional literary reference. This erasure of the past exemplifies Mircea Eliade's definition of contemporary poetic creation. The act of poetic conception for Eliade is akin to mythmaking in that both seek to recover a "primordial situation ": "But poetic creation, like linguistic creation, implies the abolition of time—of history concentrated in language—and tends towards the recovery of the paradisiac, primordial situation. . . . From a certain point of view, we may say that every great poet is *remaking* the world, for he is trying to see it as if there were no Time, no History."[15] To convey the self's primordial domain, Roethke prunes his verse of history concentrated in language. Unlike the Moderns', and especially Eliot's, use of formal rhetoric and Latin derivations to convey a poetry of meditation,

Roethke relies on words with German and Anglo-Saxon roots, as in the greenhouse poems, to dramatize regression into the unconscious.

Yet even here the dead inhabit the poet's interior dwelling, their voices echoing through the lost son's empty house. Roethke never disengages himself from the poetic tradition. That is not, finally, his aim. The double meaning of the word "gibber" conveys Roethke's ambivalence in "The Lost Son." On the one hand, gibber denotes mindless chatter, nonsense, and the purely performative dimension of linguistic usage. On the other hand, it stands for the imitative use of words. Through the poem's irrational gibber Roethke allows the echoes of precursor voices momentary surfacings in his text, only to disrupt and distort them. Roethke's use of Yeatsian imperative verbs and rhetorical questions in "The Gibber" is a case in point. In his essay "Some Remarks on Rhythm" Roethke discussed how command verbs can stimulate the reader's identification with poetic action: "We say the command, the hortatory, often makes for the memorable. We're caught up, involved" (PC, 77). Roethke further cites Yeat's work as "magnificent, often, at getting the right tone, seizing the attention" (PC, 77). To illustrate, Roethke quotes the opening imperative of "The Hawk": "Call down the hawk from the air; / Let him be hooded or caged."[16] This Yeatsian influence clearly informs Roethke's technique in "The Gibber": "Let the gestures freeze; our doom is already decided" (CP, 56).

Moreover, Roethke's rhetorical questions, that voice his awed witnessing of interior apocalypse, derive from Yeats in works such as "The Second Coming": "And what rough beast, its hour come round at last, / Slouches toward Bethlehem to be born?" (YVE, 402). But whereas Yeats uses traditional and archetypal symbols to dramatize a collective historical vision, Roethke depicts his private psychic revelation in a more personal and colloquial idiom. In fact, Roethke's surrealistic images are so idiosyncratic that, at times, his language frustrates any critical attempts to assign it determinate meaning. Moreover, many of his rhetorical questions, used to dramatize regression into the unconscious, are based on children's nonsense verse and Mother Goose rhymes that verge on verbal tautologies. Often in "The Lost Son" linguistic gesture supersedes idea, morality, or belief. As poet, Roethke recreates for his readers the strange confusion and wonder that characterize his own contact with the unconscious. His surrealistic verse invites the reader to fathom the disorder of its fragmented style through critical acts of interpretation.

In contrast to the chaotic verbal style of "The Gibber," the fifth and final section of "The Lost Son" features communion with High Modernist precursors through a more coherent dialogue. Here Eliot becomes Roethke's paternal mentor whose verbal echoes layer the poet's utterances. Several critics have remarked on the similarities between this section of "The Lost Son" and Eliot's poetic style, characteristic imagery, and diction.[17] The blend of repetition and paradox in "East Coker"—"We must be still and still moving" (CPE, 129)—also shapes Roethke's poetic gestures featuring irony and contradiction: "Stillness becoming alive / Yet still?" (CP, 58). Roethke bases his composition of place—"It was beginning winter, / An in-between time" (CP, 58)—on Eliot's intersection of two temporal orders both in "East Coker"—"In my beginning is my ending" (CPE, 123)—and "Little Gidding"—"In the dark time of the year. Between melting and freezing" (CPE, 138). Even the final visitation of Roethke's Other, the "lively understandable spirit," finds its counterpart in Eliot's communion with the "compound ghost" of his "dead master" in "Little Gidding"—"I was still the same, / Knowing myself yet being someone other" (CPE, 141).

Unlike the vacillating attitude toward paternal

figures in "The Gibber," by the close of "The Lost Son" Roethke has come to terms with his literary precursors. The regressive retreat into the unconscious has resolved Roethke's negative rivalry with past poets. Now having undergone the individuation process, Roethke awakens to the power of his own literary identity. In "The Lost Son" meaning comes as "dramatic revelation" whenever the poet enacts a moment of confrontation with the influence of the past. "The lively understandable spirit" for whom the poet waits at the close of "The Lost Son" is finally the inspiring force of his own poetic promise.

Roethke conceived "The Lost Son" as part of a larger process of poetic individuation that in 1948 included three other long works published in section 4 of *The Lost Son* volume: "The Long Alley," "A Field of Light," and "The Shape of the Fire." In a letter to Babette Deutsch dated January 22, 1948, he described "The Lost Son" as "only the first of four experiences, each in a sense stages in a kind of struggle out of the slime; part of a slow spiritual progress if you will; part of an effort to be born."[18] Each of these four poems is defined by roughly the same pattern of regression and return that organizes "The Lost Son."

These three companion-pieces to "The Lost

Son" are shaped by similar poetic techniques that structure his masterwork. Here the poet features his characteristic vegetal, subhuman imagery; the locales of earth, water, wind, and fire; the imagery of spiritual darkness and ecstatic splendor; the contrarieties of sensuous and sacred vision; and the stylistic yoking of tentative questioning and affirmative imperatives. Significantly, in a notebook entry dated from this time, Roethke's associative chain of images reflects the constituting metaphors that unify the four poems: "Greenhouse appeared in a dream as a sparkle of glass: like dream of flat water: the calm, the eye of a pond" (SF, 149). "The Long Alley" regresses back to the sensuous water scenes that are linked through the poet's unconscious associations to the greenhouse world. Thus to "Return the gaze of a pond" (CP, 59) is, for Roethke, to recollect the long alleys of the interior greenhouses.

"The Long Alley," more than "The Lost Son," works through the poet's sexual guilt to an acceptance and celebration of erotic experience. The dance of sexual euphemisms in section 3 leads to the figure of the lover "locked in / the old silo" (CP, 60) like some contemporary fairy tale princess. Section 4 culminates in the celebration of love now in the floral imagery of the long alley of the greenhouse:

THE LOST SON AND OTHER POEMS

Come littlest, come tenderest
Come whispering over the small waters,
Reach me rose, sweet one, still moist in the loam,
Come, come out of the shade, the cool ways,
The long alleys of string and stem;
Bend down, small breathers, creepers and winders;
Lean from the tiers and benches,
Cyclamen dripping and lilies.
What fish-ways you have, littlest flowers,
Swaying over the walks, in the watery air,
Drowsing in the soft light, petals pulsing. (CP, 61)

"A Field of Light" takes up the luminous presence at the field's edge that Roethke interrogates at the close of section 5 of "The Lost Son." Visual imagery here brings numinous knowledge of the eternal as Roethke explains in a journal entry dating from this period: "First I must look, then I must learn" (SF, 148). Roethke's visual communion with the splendor of the summer field climaxes in section 3 in a celebration of an August morning: "And I walked. I walked through the light air; / I moved with the morning" (CP, 63). "The Shape of the Fire," Roethke says, describes a more violent regression than either "The Lost Son" or "A Field of Light," recalling the darkest moments of "The Pit" and "The Gibber." In section 1 questions, imperatives, and direct address all heighten the intensity of Roethke's poetic estrangement:

Mother me out of here. What more will the bones
    allow?
Will the sea give the wind suck? A toad folds into a
    stone.
These flowers are all fangs. Comfort me, fury.
Wake me, witch, we'll do the dance of rotten sticks.
    (CP, 64)

Such regressive and often sexual images lead to infantile, oral associations as in "A low mouth laps water" (CP, 64). Section 2 returns to the nursery rhyme techniques of "The Flight." Here Roethke introduces images of regression to "the slime," where "the uneasy man"

> In coiling ooze
> Is trapped to the lips,
> . . . Must pull off clothes
> To jerk like a frog
> On belly and nose
> From the sucking bog. (CP, 65)

In a notebook entry from this period Roethke affirms that regression is "More than a feeling: a desire for the qualities in primitive forms of life: crabs, snails" (SF, 151). In section 3 Roethke returns to the paradox of the *via negativa*: that is, the way whereby sensual darkness leads to spiritual insight: "The journey from flesh is longest. / A rose sways least. / The redeemer comes a dark way" (CP, 66). As in "The Lost Son," the fourth and fifth sections here turn to the imagery of light and air to depict spiritual awakening out of the dark despair of mortality. Again, the closing serenity of the lake's calm surface—likened here to a vase of water that "Fills and trembles at the edge yet does not flow over" (CP, 67)—recalls the calm glass interiors that house the abundance of the garden world.

In *The Lost Son* Roethke introduced fresh subjects and innovative stylistic techniques that would shape his middle career through his *Praise to the End!* volume. His overarching concern for private and literary identity began in the greenhouse poems that regress to the locales and settings of the poet's earliest rememberings. Here Roethke discovered what would become the foundation for his distinctive subjects, symbols, and motives. The constituting metaphor of the greenhouse enabled him to merge revery with interior, psychic scenes of associative wonder. But more important, the poet's regressive descent into the primordial landscapes of the unconscious in "The Lost Son" formed the basis of an alternative poetics to Modernism's abstract, meditative rationality. Thematically, Roethke highlighted his autobiographical subjects over the collective, historical, religious, and political paradigms that shaped the writing of Eliot, Pound, and Yeats. Stylistically, the verbal techniques of surrealism provided Roethke with a resource for dramatizing his rivalry with his literary precursors. Each of the early long developmental poems of *The Lost Son* was eventually incorporated into the extended allegory of spiritual journeying that Roethke went on to explore from infancy through adolescence in his next volume *Praise to the End!*.

Notes

1. Stanley Kunitz, "Theodore Roethke, Poet of Transformations," in *Profile of Theodore Roethke*, ed. William Heyen (Columbia, MO: Charles E. Merrill, 1971) 69.

2. Louis L. Martz, "A Greenhouse Eden" in Stein, *Essays on the Poetry* 35.

3. See William Meredith, "A Steady Storm of Correspondences: Theodore Roethke's Long Journey Out of the Self," in Stein, *Essays on the Poetry* 36–53.

4. See Burke 68–108.

5. Frederick J. Hoffman, "Theodore Roethke: The Poetic Shape of Death," in Stein, *Essays on the Poetry* 94.

6. Burke 77.

7. Malkoff 52.

8. Martz 23.

9. Wallace Stevens, "The Noble Rider and the Sound of Words," *The Necessary Angel, Essays on Reality and the Imagination* (New York: Vintage Books, 1951) 35–36.

10. Mary Ann Caws, *The Poetry of Dada and Surrealism* (Princeton, NJ: Princeton University Press, 1970) 80.

11. Mircea Eliade, *Myths, Dreams and Mysteries*, trans. Philip Mairet (New York: Harper, 1967) 48.

12. Carl G. Jung, *The Collected Works of C. G. Jung*, trans. R. F. C. Hull VII (New York: Pantheon Books, 1953) 161.

13. See Harold Bloom, *The Anxiety of Influence* (New York: Oxford University Press, 1973) 142.

14. For a useful discussion of this critical controversy see Jerome Mazzaro, "Theodore Roethke and the Failures of Language" in *Profile of Theodore Roethke* 47–64.

15. Eliade 36.

16. W. B. Yeats, *The Variorum Edition of the Poems of W. B. Yeats*, ed. Peter Allt and Russell K. Alspach (New York: Macmillan, 1957) 342 (hereafter cited in the text as YVE).

17. See Jenijoy La Belle, *The Echoing Wood of Theodore Roethke* (Princeton, NJ: Princeton University Press, 1976) 102; and Roy Harvey Pearce, "Theodore Roethke: The Power of Sympathy," in Stein, *Essays on the Poetry* 183.

18. Theodore Roethke, *Selected Letters of Theodore Roethke*, ed. Ralph J. Mills, Jr. (Seattle: University of Washington Press, 1968) 140 (hereafter cited in text as SL).

CHAPTER FOUR

Praise to the End! and *The Waking*

Although "The Lost Son" was published (1948) before Roethke's third book *Praise to the End!* (1951), stylistically and thematically it belongs at the center of this volume. The *Praise to the End!* sequence grew from the four poems Roethke published together in section 4 of *The Lost Son* eventually to comprise the fourteen works grouped together as the *Praise to the End!* sequence in his 1953 collection, *The Waking*: "Where Knock Is Open Wide," "I Need, I Need," "Bring the Day!" "Give Way, Ye Gates," "Sensibility! O La!" "O Lull Me, Lull Me," "The Lost Son," "The Long Alley," A Field of Light," "The Shape of the Fire," "Praise to the End!" "Unfold! Unfold!" "I Cry, Love! Love!" and "O, Thou Opening, O." In "Open Letter" (1950) Roethke described the overarching themes that gather these works into a continuous unity. Each of these works is, he wrote, "complete in itself." But he also added that "each in a sense is

PRAISE TO THE END

a stage in a kind of struggle out of the slime; part of a slow spiritual progress to be born, and later, to become something more" (PC, 37). Later, in his 1953 BBC talk, "An American Poet Introduces Himself," Roethke said his aim in the sequence was "to trace the spiritual history of a protagonist," a kind of contemporary everyman figure for "all haunted and harried men" (PC, 10). The process of this spiritual allegory of the soul's evolution does not unfold as a coherent, linear continuum. On the contrary, Roethke's allegorical journey from "I to Otherwise" (PC, 25) is constantly detoured through his regressive aesthetic: "There is a perpetual slipping-back, then a going-forward" (PC, 39). Moreover, the sequence's formative psychic experiences "repeat themselves, thrust themselves upon us, again and again, with variation and change, each time bringing us closer to our own most particular (and thus most universal) reality" (PC, 39).

The first work in the series "Where Knock Is Open Wide" evokes the protagonist's early childhood world through the kind of nursery rhymes employed earlier in the opening sections of "The Lost Son." Critics vary as to how much significance and symbolic depth can be read into these nonsense lyrics. For his part, Roethke advised that the reader should attempt to understand them in the spirit in which they were written: that is, with the intuitive and spontaneous wonder of a child. "You will have no trouble," he said, "if you approach these poems as a child would, naively, with your whole being awake, your faculties loose and alert." But more important, Roethke stressed that they are "written to be heard, with the themes often coming alternately, as in music" (PC, 37). In its evocation of the infant's undifferentiated and prerational identification with sensual experience, "Where Knock Is Open Wide" is the most disorienting of the sequence. It "is written," Roethke said, "entirely from the viewpoint of a very small child: all interior drama; no comment, no interpretation" (PC, 41). Several of these lines employ synaesthesia, a blending of the senses, as in "God, give me a near. I hear flowers" (CP, 73), while others disrupt conventional associations and expectations as in "Sit and play / Under the rocker / Until the cows have puppies" (CP, 71). In addition, several of Roethke's childhood memories of Otto employ personification to animate the subhuman greenhouse world of the distant past:

> He watered the roses.
> His thumb had a rainbow.
> The stems said, Thank you.
> Dark came early. (CP, 73)

PRAISE TO THE END

Although these kinds of images frustrate coherent explication, Roethke's title provides a key signpost on the journey through this psychic terrain. The title is taken from a line of verse in Christopher Smart's poem "A Song to David": "And in the seat to faith assign'd, / Where ask is have, where seek is find, / Where knock is open wide."[1] According to La Belle, both poets aim to portray "a psychic state where the normal kinds of causal relationships are collapsed and where the usual disjunction between desire and gratification does not occur."[2] While Smart finds this psychic plenitude through prayer, she says, Roethke locates it in the experience of the child's experiential unity with the world. Informing Roethke's portrayal of childhood is both his intuition into what child psychology would describe as the infant's undifferentiated identification of body and world and the Romantic notion of the child's natural innocence and spiritual grace in nature, as depicted in Blake's "Songs of Innocence," Wordsworth's "Ode: Intimations of Immortality," and "My Heart Leaps Up." Like Wordsworth, Roethke's sequence assumes that "The Child is Father of the Man," whose days are "Bound each to each by natural piety."[3]

In keeping with Roethke's regressive plan, "I Need, I Need" does not advance beyond the intuitive and often chaotic imagery of "Where Knock Is

Open Wide" but continues Roethke's repetitious slipping back into early childhood experience. Stylistically, as Roethke explains in "An American Poet," the poem "opens with very oral imagery, the child's world of sucking and licking" (PC, 10). Section 2 presents the skip-rope songs and jingles of two children at play. While "I Need, I Need!" invokes the child's world, it should not be reduced to what the poet calls mere "cutesy prattle; it is not a suite in goo-goo" (PC, 41).

"Bring the Day" moves beyond the world of infancy and childhood, where, as Roethke wrote in "An American Poet," "we hear the young adolescent, half a child, then the randy young man boasting and caterwauling" (PC, 12). Here the poet depicts the protagonist's awakening to adult sexuality: "She asked her skin / To let me in: / The far leaves were for it" (CP, 77). The remaining three poems of the sequence's first section—"Give Way, Ye Gates," "Sensibility! O La!," "O Lull Me, Lull Me"—describe the adolescent's often comic but at times ecstatic opening to love and other "beginnings." Some of the images of these works are frankly erotic, set "In the high-noon of thighs" where acts of "Touch and arouse. Suck and sob" lead the protagonist into deeper identification with "the beast's heart," with "bird or a bear." Others descend into depression—to "a cold scrape in a

PRAISE TO THE END

low place"—where the poet is fated to "Curse and mourn" (CP, 80).

Each aims, as in "Sensibility! O La!" to unify the mind and body, thought and emotion, intellect and the senses, spirituality and sensuality. In other words, Roethke's general project here is to bridge the gap between such oppositions, thus returning to the kind of unified sensibility Eliot attributed to the pre-Modern, Metaphysical age of English poetry.[4] The verbal confusion of Roethke's nursery lyrics yields an improbable moment of clarity and affirmation in "O Lull Me, Lull Me"—the final poem in the first section. This work, in particular, dramatizes the poet's claim that "Dissociation often precedes a new state of clarity" (PC, 41). In answer to the first section's question "Is it time to think?" (CP 83) the poet probes at once visionary and experiential knowledge in excess of rational thought. The very elements welcome the poet's desire for unmediated communion with nature: "The air, the air provides. / Light fattens the rock" (CP, 83). Following the light's "white / Way to another grace," the poet is led into mystical identification with nature's small forms. The second section's closing lines magnify the song of creation the poet only faintly hears in section 1, now to a more euphonic intensity through the rhetorical figure of synaesthesia: "I could say hello to things;

/ I could talk to a snail; / I see what sings! / What sings!'' (CP, 84).

The second half of the *Praise to the End!* sequence, grouped after the four works of *The Lost Son* sequence, begins with the volume's title piece. Roethke takes the title "Praise to the End!" from Wordsworth's Romantic biographical epic, *The Prelude*, which like Roethke's work describes the growth and maturation of the poet's mind. The actual quote bespeaks Wordsworth's own amazement at how psychological dissociation often serves as the precondition for, as Roethke said, "a new state of clarity" (PC, 41):

> How strange that all
> The terrors, pains, and early miseries,
> Regrets, vexations, lassitudes, interfused
> Within my mind, should e'er have borne a part,
> And that a needful part, in making up
> The calm existence that is mine when I
> Am worthy of myself! Praise to the end![5]

Wordsworth asserts here that early miseries, regrets, vexations, and so on were absolutely essential, paradoxically, as rites of passage leading to self-assured moments of calm existence. Significantly, this program conforms exactly to Roethke's own biographical experience worked out in "The Lost Son."

PRAISE TO THE END

"Praise to the End!" enacts a similar reversal of estrangement leading to ecstatic joy and celebration. The poem's opening erotic act of onanism, as Roethke described it in "Open Letter," marks the nadir of the protagonist's solipsism. "There are laments for lost powers," the poet said, "and then a euphoric passage, a sublimation of the original impulse of ecstasy; but—and this is the point—in this passage the protagonist, for all his joy is still 'alone.' " Roethke summed up the whole poem as a "dead-end explored" (PC, 40); yet his protagonist survives erotic euphoria: "His self-consciousness, his very will to live saves him from the *annihilation* of the ecstasy" (PC, 40-41). The poem's final fourth section reverses its descent into pure sensation with the same imagery of spiritual singing that ends "O Lull Me, Lull Me": "I've crawled from the mire, alert as a saint or a dog / . . . I hear, clearly, the heart of another singing, / Lighter than bells, / Softer than water" (CP, 88). "Unfold! Unfold!" presents a similar dramatic transfiguration of the spirit's descent into nature by moments of what Wordsworth describes as calm existence. Here the regressive movement back to the secure but sub-human world is suddenly arrested and thrown forward into an unsettling encounter with eternity:

By snails, by leaps of frog, I came here, spirit.
Tell me, body without skin, does a fish sweat?
I can't crawl back through those veins,
I ache for another choice.
The cliffs! The cliffs! They fling me back.
Eternity howls in the last crags,
The field is no longer simple:
It's a soul's crossing time.
The dead speak noise. (CP, 89)

Negotiating the "soul's crossing time" of eternity and its muttering dead leads again to the choruses of natural revelation. The same synaesthetic blending of light and sound motifs characterizes the moment of spiritual ecstasy, where "A light song comes from the leaves. / A slow sigh says yes. And light sighs" (CP, 90). In such moments Roethke completes "the struggle out of the slime" arriving at "A house for wisdom; a field for revelation" (CP, 90).

"I Cry, Love! Love!" completes the *Praise to the End!* sequence as originally published, though Roethke later added a final work—the first lyric of *The Waking:* "O, Thou Opening, O." The title, as Jenijoy La Belle has pointed out, is taken from William Blake's *Visions of the Daughters of Albion.* There Blake distinguishes divine love from the "self-love that envies all."[6] Cosmic love leads to an expansion of perceptual understanding, while self-love constricts it. As in "O Lull Me, Lull Me," the poet again jettisons reason, "That dreary shed, that hutch for grubby schoolboys!" in favor of a more intuitive communion with "The hedgewren's song," that he affirms, "says something else" (CP, 92). That something else, as in the closing images of "The Shape of the Fire," is staged through a water metaphor, whose moment mediates inner and outer harmony: "The shine on the face of the lake / Tilts, backward and forward" (CP, 93). Now regression and progression, the self's retreat back into the psyche and its movement outward toward nature, are no longer at odds with one another but become reconciled in the poet's mature craft.

Similarly, "O, Though Opening, O," the final work in this sequence, enacts a complementary vision through the fusion of opposites. In the poet's quest to "Hear the sigh of what is," he returns to the wildly associative verbal techniques, the "psychic shorthand," that shape the whole sequence. Striking maxims bespeaking the merging of polar extremes—as in "The Depth calls to the Height" (CP, 97), or "The dark has its own light" (CP, 98)—sum up the harmony each of these developmental poems aims to achieve.

Roethke's next volume, *The Waking*, winner of the Pulitzer Prize, is thematically continuous with the *Praise to the End!* sequence. The book's title piece, in particular, encapsulates the theme of the earlier sequence leaning toward intuitive, emotive, and irrational modes of experience: "We think by feeling," the poet writes, "What is there to know?" (CP, 108). Moreover, Roethke presents this kind of emotive knowledge through the mystical fusion of opposites depicted in "O, Thou Opening, O." "Sleep" yields "waking"; "shaking" keeps the poet "steady"; "What falls away" "is near," and so on.

Reiterating the theme of psychic regression, Roethke's journey out of the self once again begins with an identification with the least aspects of nature's subhuman world both in the poet's exclamatory utterance "God Bless the Ground!" and his care to "walk softly there." Likewise, the "lowly worm," paradoxically, "climbs up a winding stair" (CP, 108). Roethke may have borrowed this traditional emblem of spiritual ascent from Yeats's "Dialogue of Self and Soul," where the soul summons the self to ascend another "winding ancient stair" (YVE, 477). Although "The Waking" does not enact in detail the process of spiritual journeying shaping the long developmental pieces of *Praise to the End!*, the poem nonetheless compresses it thematically in lines such as: "I feel my fate in what I cannot fear" and the refrain line, "I learn by going where I have to go" (CP, 108).

THE WAKING

Although thematically akin to the *Praise to the End!* poems, *The Waking* collection marks a radical departure in form and style, looking back to the formalist works of the poet's first volume. Unlike the free verse interior monologues of the earlier long poems, "The Waking" is composed in a complex closed form, the villanelle. This ornate, fixed form gathers its force from the first and third lines of the initial tercet that alternate as refrain lines at the close of each of the poem's remaining four tercets, climaxing in their final repetition in the closing quatrain: "I wake to sleep, and take my waking slow. . . . / I learn by going where I have to go" (CP, 108). The poem enacts a gradual revelation of the truth of these maxims through building powerful examples in each of the stanzaic units.

In addition to this masterful villanelle, Roethke's controversial formalist sequence "Four for Sir John Davies" stands in sharp contrast to his earlier open-form work. In this sequence, Roethke employs six-line iambic pentameter stanzas rhyming *ababcc* with a high proportion of end-stopped lines, making for dramatically memorable statements. Formative influences that tend to dominate the sequence include the Elizabethan poets Sir John Davies and Sir Walter Raleigh, and Roethke's twentieth-century precursor W. B. Yeats. In teaching creative writing, the poet used their works as models for poetic imitation. Roethke's frank admission of his borrowings in "The Dance"—"I take this cadence from a man named Yeats" (CP, 105)—has led several critics to dismiss these pieces as mere exercises, almost totally derivative of earlier poems.[7]

In approaching this controversial sequence one should understand the sources the poems presuppose. The opening work "The Dance," as several of Roethke's critics have pointed out, is based on a work by Sir John Davies entitled "Orchestra, or a Poem on Dancing." As La Belle shows, Davies also invokes past writers such as Virgil, Chaucer, Sidney, and Spenser, not so much in imitation as a reaffirmation of his poetic heritage. Roethke's opening question probes whether the Western humanistic tradition is still plausible for the Modern period:

Is that dance slowing in the mind of man
That made him think the universe could hum?
The great wheel turns its axle when it can;
I need a place to sing, and dancing-room,
And I have made a promise to my ears
I'll sing and whistle romping with the bears. (CP, 105)

Roethke's reference to the dance and hum of the universe alludes to Elizabethan cosmology. For a sixteenth-century poet like Davies, the cosmos revolved about the earth according to the cosmic plan of the Ptolemaic universe: in spiritual spheres of order whose music or hum witnessed to the divine harmony of the Creator: "For all the world's great fortunes and affaires / Forward and backward rapt and whirled are / According to the musicke of the spheares."[8] Roethke's poem moves beyond mere imitation as he questions whether, or in what terms, Davies's poem of dancing still speaks to the Modern age. Roethke's assertion that "I need a place to sing, and dancing room" bespeaks more than a personal necessity as it is joined to the last couplet's astrological gloss: the poet's desire to "sing and whistle romping with the bears." The bear imagery here is not fortuitous but alludes to Davies's own reference to the bear constellations Ursa Major and Ursa Minor. The poet's desire for dancing room and song ultimately answers the opening question by affirming the Modern age's continuing need for new patterns or "dances" of cosmic order. The poem draws its force, in part, from the recollection of a time without song or dance when the "blood leaped with a wordless song." The experience of the failure of imaginative expression leads to the conviction that "dancing" as the poet says "needs a master" (CP, 105). Finally, in the concluding stanza Roethke admits that for him that master is Yeats.

In some sense, Roethke took his poetic apprenticeship to the former writer literally, confessing to a moment of psychic communion with the dead poet: "Suddenly, in the early evening, the poem 'The Dance' started, and finished itself in a very short time—say thirty minutes, maybe in the greater part of an hour; it was all done. . . . But at the same time I had, as God is my witness, the actual sense of a Presence—as if Yeats himself were *in* that room. . . . At last I was somebody again. He, they—the poets dead—were with me" (PC, 24). Roethke's ecstatic communion confirms the poem's maxim that all dancing needs a master. The poet's biographical admission to the creative, even metaphysical, power of influence reinforces the poem's affirmation of the importance of dialogue with literary tradition. Such influence transcends imitation as a vital transmission of values, meanings, and ultimately a writer's literary identity. Moreover, the act of verse composition and the influences it encounters return the poet to himself, making him "somebody again." But equally important, the act of writing itself dispels the tone of anxious doubt registered in the poem's opening question with an excess of spiritual dancing—with the poet becoming "dancing-mad."

"The Partner" advances Roethke's imaginative quest for divine order inaugurated in "The

Dance," now through a thematic shift to the mystical power of sexual love. Whereas the first poem dwells on the survival of belief—"Is that dance slowing in the mind of man?"—"The Partner" interrogates the spirit's "dancing madness" further by seeking to answer the question "What is desire?" Is it, the poet asks, "The impulse to make someone else complete?" And if so, by what means can one complete another? The first stanza considers sexuality as one way, invoking an image of a woman who "would set sodden straw on fire" (CP, 105). In tracing out the influences shaping the sexual conceit of "The Partner," Jay Parini situates this line and the erotic images of stanza 2—"She kissed me close, and then did something else. / My marrow beat as wildly as my pulse" (CP, 106)—in the tradition of mystical eroticism of the Old Testament's Song of Solomon, Spenser's *Ode to Heavenly Beauty,* and Milton's justification of "earthly love as a means for ascending to heavenly love."[9]

The dance of the spirit, for Roethke, can only be done with a partner. This can be understood not only in terms of pure sensuality but also psychologically through Jung's notion of the union or integration of the poet's "animus," or masculine half of the psyche, with his "anima," or feminine side. For her part, Edith Underhill, a crucial source for Roethke's thoughts on spirituality, explains that the image of the love "partners" is a mystical symbol of cosmic love. "It was natural," she writes, "and inevitable that the imagery of human love and marriage should have seemed to the mystic the best of all images of his own 'fulfillment of life'; his soul's surrender, first to the call, finally to the embrace of Perfect Love."[10] In terms of the poem's imagery of love, union with the partner regresses back into the sensual world of nature, the subhuman, and the secret life of things that Roethke characteristically depicts in the imagery of redemptive darkness: "The body and the soul," he affirms, "know how to play / In that dark world where gods have lost their way" (CP, 106).

"The Wraith" further blends the imagery of spiritual communion with erotic love as the poet recollects how "The spirit and the flesh cried out for more." Here Roethke probes for a plausible answer to the question concerning, again, the sacred union of opposites: "Did each become the other in that play?" (CP, 106). This question recalls Yeats's similar rhetorical question in "Leda and the Swan": "Did she [Leda] put on his [Zeus's] knowledge with his power" (YVE, 441). Both poets question whether sexuality yields spiritual knowledge. In stanza 2 moments of playful eroticism occur—"In the deep middle of ourselves we lay"—and lead in stanza 3 to the more mystical claim that

THE WAKING

"The flesh can make the spirit visible" (CP, 106). Predictably, Roethke here likens the grace of reconciled opposites to the Romantic innocence of childhood: "We played with dark and light as children should" (CP, 107).

Such regression, in turn, leads in stanza 4 to deeper questioning of the soul's sensual incarnations:

> What shape leaped forward at the sensual cry?—
> Sea-beast or bird flung toward the ravaged shore?
> Did space shake off an angel with a sigh?
> We rose to meet the moon, and saw no more.
> It was and was not she, a shape alone,
> Impaled on light, and whirling slowly down.
>   (CP, 107)

Here the sensual cry of sexual union yields a tentative visionary fusion of opposites. The lover both "was and was not she" imbued with an otherness the poet describes variously as the shape of a "sea-beast or bird," or "angel." Both seeing "no more" and "impaled on light," the lovers' paradoxical vision—enacted here in the poem's climatic moment—eludes Roethke's insistent questioning.

"The Vigil" sums up the sequence's various motifs and themes by again considering the adequacy of sexual love as a literal metaphor for mystical union. Specifically, Roethke invokes

Dante's spiritual journey and mystical love for Beatrice as the poetic prototype for the celebration of his own Beatrice O'Connell, whom he married in 1953:

> Dante attained the purgatorial hill,
> Trembled at hidden virtue without flaw,
> Shook with a mighty power beyond his will,—
> Did Beatrice deny what Dante saw?
> All lovers live by longing, and endure:
> Summon a vision and declare it pure. (CP, 107)

Meditating on Dante's sojourn in hell, his endurance of purgatory, and final vision of "hidden virtue without flaw," Roethke poses the question that is crucial for his own sequence of love poems: "Did Beatrice deny what Dante saw?" The rest of the poem attempts an answer that will justify earthly love in spiritual terms. Significantly, while mystical vision is something the lovers summon, it must be proved by the poet who will "declare it pure." That is, the moment of sexual love's transfiguration into cosmic terms is at once actual and fictive.

Roethke's celebration of Beatrice returns to the luminous imagery of spiritual ecstasy: "The waves broke easy, cried to me in white; / Her look was morning in the dying light." Love as a kind of "supreme fiction" is something the lovers create,

old lady was once "sweet with the light of myself /
A self-delighting creature" (CP, 103). Now, however, this poem's persona no longer embodies
self-delighting joy but instead anticipates the after-
life:

> O for some minstrel of what's to be
> A bird singing into the beyond,
> The marrow of God, talking,
> Full merry, a gleam
> Gracious and bland,
> On a bright stone. (CP, 103)

Although this work is not particularly memorable
in the Roethke canon and largely overlooked by his
critics, the poet's austere winter setting and his
persona's longing for spiritual renewal—"My dust
longs for the invisible" (CP, 104)—anticipate later
ruminations on death's transcendence in such poems as "The Dying Man" and "Meditations of an
Old Woman" from *Words for the Wind* and several
of his long poems and metaphysical lyrics from the
posthumously published volume *The Far Field*.

Roethke's middle career builds on *The Lost
Son*'s emerging aesthetic by advancing the poet's
reliance on pastoral subjects and depth psychology. Ranging from the irrational, nonsense verse
of "Where Knock Is Open Wide" through the
emotive and often mystical awakenings of "O,

UNDERSTANDING THEODORE ROETHKE

Thou Opening, O," the *Praise to the End!* sequence presents a sustained meditation on the self's progress from childhood to adulthood. Advancing beyond this developmental sequence, *The Waking* marks a pivotal point in Roethke's career in several ways. Returning to the poet's early formalist style in *Open House*, works such as "Four for Sir John Davies" and "The Waking" manifest the poet's mastery of fixed forms. Thematically, Roethke's fascination with the contrarieties of experience, his exploration of sexuality as a catalyst for mystical knowledge, his use of feminine portraits and personae, and his growing concern for the sacred set the terms for his mature writing throughout his later career.

Notes

1. Christopher Smart, *The Religious Poetry of Christopher Smart*, ed. Marcus Walsh (Oxford: Carcanet Press, 1972) 70; cited in La Belle 52.

2. La Belle 53.

3. William Wordsworth, *Poems, in Two Volumes, and Other Poems*, ed. Jaren Curtis (Ithaca, NY: Cornell University Press, 1983) 206.

4. See T. S. Eliot, "The Metaphysical Poets," in *Selected Essays* (New York: Harcourt Brace, 1960) 241–50.

5. William Wordsworth, *The Fourteen-Book Prelude*, ed. W. J. B. Owen (Ithaca, NY: Cornell University Press, 1985) 37.

6. William Blake cited by La Belle 106.

7. See W. D. Snodgrass, " 'That Anguish of Concreteness'—Theodore Roethke's Career," in *Theodore Roethke: Essays on the Poetry* 78–93; and Stephen Spender, "The Objective Ego," in Stein, *Essays on the Poetry* 3–13.

8. Sir John Davies, *Orchestra, or a Poem of Dancing* (Middlesex, England: Stanton Press, 1922) 30.

9. Parini 142.

10. Evelyn Underhill, *Mysticism: A study in the nature and development of Man's spiritual consciousness* (NY: Meridian Books, 1955) 136.

11. Parini 138.

CHAPTER FIVE

Words for the Wind

Reflecting back on his marriage to Beatrice O'Connell five years earlier, *Words for the Wind* (1958) deepens Roethke's identification with feminine partners undertaken in *The Waking*. The poet's devotion to Beatrice culminates in his second section of "Love Poems" and, in particular, with his volume's title piece. "The poem," Roethke said, "is an epithalamion to a bride seventeen years younger."[1] An epithalamion is a bridal song that celebrates the occasion of a wedding, whose tradition goes back to Pindar, Sappho, Theocritus, and Catullus. Spenser's *Epithalamion* with its floral passages and praise for both the physical and spiritual beauty of the bride is perhaps a literary model for Roethke's own celebration of Beatrice. Marriage opens the poet to a new range of experience and poetic subjects: "I was able to move outside myself," he wrote, "for me sometimes a violent dislocation—and express a joy in another, in others": I mean Beatrice O'Connell."[2] Roethke's love poems, like his earlier formalist sequence "Four for Sir John Davies," comprise at once the poet's secular and mystical understanding of love, again fusing sensual and spiritual experience into a unified vision.

From his readings in Evelyn Underhill's *Mysticism*, Roethke was aware of the imagery of love and marriage as symbols in mystical literature for the soul's attunement to God. While influenced by Underhill's writings on mystical love, Roethke depicts the spiritual and psychic dimensions of secular desire in his own characteristic terms. In portraying his complex understanding of love, the poet returns to themes, motifs, and poetic usages from the earliest moments of his career:

> Love, love, a lily's my care,
> She's sweeter than a tree.
> Loving, I use the air
> Most lovingly: I breathe;
> Mad in the wind I wear
> Myself as I should be. (CP, 123)

The images of lily, vine, and tree describe the nurturing of love as a delicate art of "care," reminiscent of the vocation of the greenhouse magicians of *The Lost Son*. The depiction of love's euphoria as a kind of madness returns to the confessional thematics and language of *Open House*. Compare, for example "I wear / Myself as I should be," with the poet's earlier assertion from his first volume's title piece: "Myself is what I wear" (CP, 3). In both works, the most intimate of the self's confessional experiences, visionary moments, and spiritual insights are featured as explicit poetic materials. These visionary love lyrics, therefore, continue the confessional program of Roethke's earliest writings, where, as he says, "My secrets cry aloud" (CP, 3).

Advancing the complementary vision of the *Praise to the End!* sequence of his middle career, Roethke complicates his personal confessionalism with the more uncanny and cosmic merging of opposites that he read variously in Evelyn Underhill and English and German Romantic verse. "All's even," he says, "with the odd" (CP, 123). Just as the poet's "shaking" keeps him "steady" in "The Waking," so here "Motion," he says "can keep me still" (CP, 123). As in "The Dream" and "The Visitant" from *The Waking*, the figure of the lover blurs the boundary dividing the interior psyche from the exterior world, becoming one with the poet's own anima, or feminine side: "A shape from deep in the eye— / That woman I saw in a stone— / Keeps pace when I walk alone" (CP, 123).

WORDS FOR THE WIND

The poem's second section further explores images that invest the physical world with love's joyful aura. Settings of expansive openness to nature as in stanza 1's wide plain, field, and sea imagery are compressed in the synecdochic figures of stanza 2—the dove, rose, and vine. Through oxymoron, the section ends with a surplus of joy here describing Roethke's palpable ecstasy as a kind of emotional burden: "I bear," he writes, "but not alone / The burden of this joy" (CP, 124). The poem's third section moves from the spatial settings of section 2 to a meditation on love's persistence in time:

> Wisdom, where is it found?—
> Those who embrace, believe.
> Whatever was, still is,
> Says a song tied to a tree.
> Below, on the ferny ground,
> In rivery air, at ease,
> I walk with my true love. (CP, 125)

Love's moment abides as an eternal present that brings the lovers into edenic contact with the pastoral world. Such idyllic grace, celebrated in "a song tied to a tree," recalls the natural choruses that sing to the poet throughout the visionary moments of the *Praise to the End!* sequence. Moreover, echoing "The Waking" and the fortunate fall into nature's kingdom—"What falls away is al-

ways. And is near." (CP, 108)—Roethke writes,
"What falls away will fall; / All things bring me to
love" (CP, 125).

Section 4 summarizes the poem's themes and
images beginning with a catalogue of subtle and
obscure natural personifications that "wakes the
ends of life" (CP, 125). Sexuality in stanza 2, as "a
thing / Body and spirit know" (CP, 126), elevates
the physical world into a mystic state in the poem's
final lines:

> And I dance round and round,
> A fond and foolish man,
> And see and suffer myself
> In another being, at last. (CP, 126)

Employing an earlier conceit from "Four for Sir
John Davies," Roethke presents the physical act of
love-making as an ecstatic dance leading beyond
the self as he says in "On 'Identity' ": "from I to
Otherwise, or maybe even to Thee" (PC, 25).

Words for the Wind encapsulates themes and
images elaborated at length throughout earlier sequences. "The Dream," like "The Visitant," for
example, expands the psychic correspondence between the outward lover and the inward anima as
the flowering of an intuitive oneness: "I met her as
a blossom on a stem / Before she ever breathed,
and in that dream / The mind remembers from a
deeper sleep" (CP, 119). In addition, the same light

and fire imagery Roethke employs throughout *The Waking* to depict love's spiritual aura predominates in the controlling symbolism of "The Dream": "She came toward me in the flowing air, / A shape of change, encircled by its fire" (CP, 119). Like "Words for the Wind," "The Dream" successfully combines striking imagery and memorable lyric utterances such as "Love is not love until love's vulnerable" (CP, 120).

The "Love Poems" sequence comprises both sensual and mystical appreciations of love. "I Knew a Woman" and "The Sensualists," for example, are candidly erotic, recalling the sexual knowledge Roethke discovers in the *Praise to the End!* sequence. Such works at times recall through their comic irony the metaphysical wit of seventeenth-century English love lyrics as in "The Swan": "I am my father's son, I am John Donne / Whenever I see her with nothing on" (CP, 140). "I Knew a Woman," in particular, employs the imagery of English pastoral verse as in Marvell's "mower" poems: "She was the sickle; I, poor I, the rake, / Coming behind her for her pretty sake / (But what prodigious mowing we did make)" (CP, 127). Following Eliot's earlier reading of the Metaphysical poets, Roethke was drawn to their unity of sensual perception and intellect that, according to Eliot, became "dissociated" in the Modern age: "The metaphysical poet," Roethke wrote, " . . . thinks with his body: an idea for him can be as real as the smell of a flower or a blow on the head. And those so lucky as to bring their whole sensory equipment to bear on the process of thought grow faster, jump more frequently from one plateau to another more often" (PC, 27).

Similarly, "The Sententious Man" aims to recover through erotic love the Metaphysical poet's fusion of sensation and thought where "Spirit and nature beat in one breast-bone" (CP, 131). Instead of weighing the soul down, flesh here feeds the spirit's fiery intensity:

> We did not fly the flesh. Who does, when young?
> A fire leaps on itself: I know that flame.
> Some rages save us. Did I rage too long?
> The spirit knows the flesh it must consume. (CP, 131)

The same imagery of spiritual fire is employed again in section 3 in the portrayal of sexual union: "There was a thicket where I went to die, / And there I thrashed, my thighs and face aflame." The word "die," which in Metaphysical and Elizabethan verse often refers to sexual climax, leads to a celebration of cosmic unity: "But my least motion changed into a song, / And all dimensions quivered to one thing" (CP, 132).

"The Pure Fury," "The Renewal," and "Love's Progress" move beyond this kind of mystified eroticism to test love's endurance of death, despair, and nothingness:

> The pure admire the pure, and live alone;
> I love a woman with an empty face.
> Parmenides put Nothingness in place;
> She tries to think, and it flies loose again.
> How slow the changes of a golden mean:
> Great Boehme rooted all in Yes and No;
> At times my darling squeaks in pure Plato. (CP, 133)

As Roethke's opening implies, spiritual purity is refined by solitude and further through acknowledging moments of what Paul Tillich describes as non-being in *The Courage to Be*. In fact, Roethke's catalogue of philosphers who theorized nothingness, as the poet's critics have shown, is itself based on a passage he read in Tillich:

Non-being is one of the most difficult and most discussed concepts. Parmenides tried to remove it as a concept. But in order to do so he had to sacrifice life. Democritos re-established it and identified it with empty space, in order to make movement thinkable. Plato used the concept of non-being because without it the contrast of existence with pure essences is beyond understanding. It is implied in Aristotle's distinction between matter and form. . . . Jacob Boehme, the Protestant mystic and philosopher of life, made the classical statement that all things are rooted in a Yes and a No.[3]

The poet preserves love's intensity and power, paradoxically, by acknowledging his "terrible . . . need for solitude" (CP, 133). Likewise, spiritual illumination emerges out of the palpable darkness of the abyss of non-being: "I live near the abyss. I hope to stay / Until my eyes look at a brighter sun / As the thick shade of the long night comes on" (CP, 134).

The poet's existential descent into nothingness continues throughout the rest of the love sequence returning to the landscape of psychic bewilderment and spiritual testing in "The Lost Son." In "The Renewal," "Dark hangs upon the waters of the soul" as Roethke once again returns to the anxious questioning of "The Lost Son": "Does my father live?" (CP, 135). But the lost self survives the "midnight air," thereby witnessing in section 4 to redemptive illumination: "As if reality had split apart," he says, "And the whole motion of the soul lay bare: / I find that love, and I am everywhere" (CP, 135). The knowledge of one's own personal finitude is the ultimate truth for Roethke. The poet continually faces up to his own mortality even as it taints the entire world with the angst of nothingness. By the end of "Love Poems" in *Words for the Wind* Roethke has returned to the regressive wisdom of his *Praise to the End!* sequence:

WORDS FOR THE WIND

> I lived with deep roots once:
> Have I forgotten their ways—
> The gradual embrace
> Of lichen around stones?
> Death is a deeper sleep,
> And I delight in sleep. (CP, 139)

The third section of *Words for the Wind*, as Roethke described it in a late essay, "consists of poems of terror, and running away—and the dissociation of personality that occurs in such attempts to escape reality. In these the protagonist is alive in space, almost against his will; his world is the cold and dark known to sub-human things" (PC, 58). The poet's entrapment in a world described in terms of darkness and terror is memorably captured in the refrain of "The Shimmer of Evil": "There was no light; there was no light at all." The outer scene of spiritual emptiness where "Cold evil twinkled tighter than a string" (CP, 143) is internalized in "Elegy" as the poet's "inner weight of woe" (CP, 144). These unbearable terms of existence, nevertheless, define the precondition for testing the poet's imaginative courage: "Father of flowers," he asks, "who / Dares face the thing he is?" (CP, 147). Roethke proves himself worthy of this challenge through accepting his identity with the subhuman as in "The Small," "Snake," and "Slug." "Exorcism," in particular, enacts an unset-

tling encounter with nature's simple lives here
presented as demonic emblems of self-knowledge:

> In a dark wood I saw—
> I saw my several selves
> Come running from the leaves,
> Lewd, tiny, careless lives
> That scuttled under stones,
> Or broke, but would not go. (CP, 147)

Such necessary acknowledgments of the several selves of the poet's secret life lead to redemptive moments, depicting the purged soul's
correspondence with nature as in the closing image
of "A Walk in Late Summer": "Beyond the ridge
two wood thrush sing as one. / Being delights in
being, and in time. / The evening wraps me, steady
as a flame" (CP, 150). The poet's recognition of his
own slow mortality—"I'm dying piecemeal; fer-
vent in decay" (CP, 149)—anticipates Roethke's
extended meditations on death in his formalist
poem dedicated to W. B. Yeats "The Dying Man"
and his long open-form poem "Meditations of an
Old Woman."

Unlike the subhuman imagery of mortal despair Roethke employs in the poems of section 3,
"The Dying Man" relies more on lyric statement
compressed into frequently end-stopped lines of
iambic trimeter of the first two parts and

pentamenter of parts three through five. The poem
opens onto the moment of death as poised on the
threshold between the earthly and the Eternal: "I
know, as the dying know, / Eternity is Now. . . . A
man sees, as he dies, / Death's possibilities" (CP,
153). Section 2, "What Now?" further probes those
possibilities as rebirth into future incarnations:
"Caught in the dying light, / I thought myself
reborn. / My hands turn into hooves" (CP, 154).
Section 3, "The Wall," describes through metaphor
the barrier variously separating the living from the
dead, the conscious mind from the unconscious
psyche, the present from the past, the dawn from
the dark, and the "pure image" from the sensual
eye.

Images of the father haunt this section; as the
poet says, "I found my father when I did my work,
/ Only to lose myself in this small dark" (CP, 154).
Otto reappears as "the dying man" again in section
4, "The Exulting," in recollections of the father's
slow, painful demise from cancer: "Was it a god his
suffering renewed?— / I saw my father shrinking in
his skin" (CP, 155). Beyond viewing death through
the poetic masks of Yeats and his father, Roethke
himself is the subject of "The Dying Man." Death
becomes one with life through the poet's vital acts
of social and psychic survival: "My enemies renew
me, and my blood / Beats slower in my careless

solitude. / I bare a wound, and dare myself to bleed" (CP, 155). But unlike the dance of light that Roethke performs in "Four for Sir John Davies," in the fifth section of "The Dying Man," "They Sing, They Sing," the music of heaven's orchestra is intoned "in minor thirds" of descent into "the immense immeasurable emptiness of things." The poet more deeply questions his own non-being in the face of death: "Am I but nothing," he asks, "leaning toward a thing?" Neither the secret life of things is entirely redemptive, "Nor can imagination do it all / In this last place of light" (CP, 156). Moreover, love is reduced to but "a motion in the mind," that is itself infected by emptiness. Significantly, the fifth and final section of "The Dying Man" invokes another dancing partner now as muse for celebrating the poet's negative vision of eternity: "All women loved dance in a dying light— / The moon's my mother: how I love the moon!" (CP, 156). "The Dying Man" 's final appeal to female personae looks forward to the poet's long open-form "Meditations of an Old Woman," the fifth and last sequence of *Words for the Wind.*

Roethke quests for a unified sensibility in both his open-form love poems and the lyric formalism of "The Dying Man," based in sixteenth-century poetic forms. Both parts of *Words for the Wind* culminate in section 5, "Meditations of an Old

WORDS FOR THE WIND

Woman." This narrative mask Roethke revealed in "Theodore Roethke Writes . . . " was "modelled in part," he said, "after my own mother . . . in other words, a gentle, highly articulate old lady believing in the glories of the world; yet fully conscious of its evils" (PC, 58). Roethke chose a poetic persona who is worldly, sophisticated, well-read, and yet gentle in her responsiveness to the subtle presences and beings of the natural world. In other words, she embodies the kind of fusion of intellect, emotion, and perception that Roethke prized in Metaphysical verse.

The various levels of her meditations can be grouped under three broad rubrics—self, heart (memory), and soul—as Roethke sums them up in his final section: "The self says, I am; / The heart says, I am less; / The spirit says, you are nothing" (CP, 172). The self can be considered as situated on the border between life and death, past and present, the conscious and unconscious, the spiritual life and sensuous existence. Here the old woman asks "How can I rest in the days of my slowness?" (CP, 157). That is, what manner of being in the world or posture toward experience will enable her to say as the self "I am." The self's journey begins in its aloneness: "I was always one for being alone," she says, "Seeking in my own way, eternal purpose" (CP, 168). Although she achieves the necessary solitude that Roethke says is a precondition for spiritual vision in "The Pure Fury," she is a "Perpetual beginner" whose "soul knows not what to believe" (CP, 171). The progress of Roethke's long developmental poems of "spiritual journeying" begins in the solipsism of "self-involvement," moving tentatively "from I to Otherwise" (PC, 25). Exploiting solitude, paradoxically, in order to get outside the confines of the self's ego, the old woman realizes that "I need an old crone's knowing" (CP, 157). That knowledge initially comprises the heart's wisdom, the accumulated experience of feminine memory.

Her journey toward viewing herself "Otherwise" begins "on a bus through western country" anticipating Roethke's car trips through the American West in "Journey to the Interior" of "North American Sequence." Here the journey regresses "Backward in time" through a "Journey within a journey" (CP, 158): that is, through memory with all its adventures, "inaccessible" "gates" and detoured paths. In "I'm Here" the old woman recollects her former selves, registering the same tones of exuberant joy in nature that characterize the reveries on youth and adolescence in "Old Lady's Winter Words":

WORDS FOR THE WIND

> I was queen of the vale—
> For a short while,
> Living all my heart's summer alone,
> Ward of my spirit,
> Running through high grasses,
> My thighs brushing against flower-crowns;
> Leaning, out of breath,
> Bracing my back against a sapling,
> Making it quiver with my body. (CP, 161)

As "queen of the vale— / For a short while" the young girl inhabits the same idyllic realm of natural magic that Dylan Thomas celebrates in "Fern Hill." Her youthful vigor—captured in Roethke's participial verbs "living," "running," "brushing," "leaning," "bracing," and "rubbing"—along with the stanza's pastoral imagery recall Roethke's earlier presentation of girlhood in "Elegy for Jane."

Moving beyond the adolescent's natural grace, Roethke anticipates later feminist writing centered on women's experience, as in the poetry of Sylvia Plath, Adrienne Rich, and Anne Sexton. Although critics have rightly pointed out the stereotypic and sentimental quality of Roethke's images of women, in "Meditations" his feminine persona is more plausible. "Perhaps inevitably," writes Anthony Libby, "Roethke's most forceful and enlightened woman is not the figure of a lover but an intelligent

mother-figure.''[4] Significantly, "Fourth Meditation" lodges a poignant critique of women's alien-
ated place within postwar American culture.
Following Whitman's question in section 20 of
"Song of Myself"—"What is a man anyhow? What
am I? what are you?"[5]—Roethke asks "What is it to
be a woman?" (CP, 169):

> I think of the self-involved:
> The ritualists of the mirror, the lonely drinkers,
> The minions of benzedrine and paraldehyde,
> And those who submerge themselves deliberately in
> trivia,
> Women who become their possessions,
> Shapes stiffening into metal,
> Match-makers, arrangers of picnics—
> What do their lives mean,
> And the lives of their children?— (CP, 169)

Tragically determined by America's male-oriented
postwar society, women's available roles here are
frivolous, trivial, narcissistic, and worthless. Like
Eliot's "Hollow Men," Roethke's domestic women
of the 1950s are reduced to the status of the
possessions they accumulate. Writing before the
social, political, and economic agendas of the feminist movement of the 1960s, Roethke's solution to
women's alienation under patriarchal society
seems somewhat idealistic. The poet's regression
into natural innocence is a well-intentioned but

overly simplistic answer to a complex cultural problem:

May the high flower of the hay climb into their hearts
May they lean into light and live;
May they sleep in robes of green, among the ancient
    ferns
. . . May they be taken by the true burning;
May they flame into being!" (CP, 169)

Ultimately, the memory of other women's lives can only offer a partial and compromised fulfillment for Roethke's feminine persona.

Now sequestered in the greenhouse world of "The Lost Son," the old woman realizes that "My geranium," another of Roethke's floral emblems for the soul, "is dying, for all I can do" (CP, 163). Like the lost son, she must make the spiritual journey "from I to Otherwise" beyond the glass-house and out to "the edge of the field waiting for the pure moment" (CP, 168). Through the duet two song sparrows sing in "First Meditation," Roethke dramatizes the need to integrate what is inside the greenhouse—his constituting metaphor for the self—with what is outside and other to it. The goal of the old woman's meditations is to achieve this harmonious reciprocity between the life within and without, between the self and nature. Deeply in touch with the organic life of things, Roethke's old woman leans toward the kind of animistic mysticism the poet describes in "On 'Identity' ": "If the dead can come to our aid in a quest for identity, so can the living—and I mean *all* living things, including the sub-human. This is not so much a naive as a primitive attitude: animistic maybe. Why Not? Everything that lives is holy: I call upon those holy forms of life" (PC, 24).

Whereas the "Love Poems" of *Words for the Wind* employ the mystical metaphor of the lovers to depict the poet's spiritual understanding, "Meditations" returns to the *Praise to the End!* metaphor of the animistic journey through nature, the psyche, and memory to dramatize the progress of the soul. "The spirit moves," she says in "First Meditation," "but not always upward" (CP, 157). Instead, the self's sojourn is regressive, returning to Roethke's guiding dictum that "the spiritual man must go back in order to go forward" (PC, 12). Roethke describes this facility to shuttle backward and forward between self and nature, life and death, the personal psyche and the collective unconscious by borrowing a key metaphor from Walt Whitman's "Out of the Cradle Endlessly Rocking":

> The body, delighting in thresholds,
> Rocks in and out of itself,
> A bird, small as a leaf,
> Sings in the first
> Sunlight. (CP, 163)

WORDS FOR THE WIND

Mastering Whitman's rocking motion allows the old woman "to be delivered from the rational into the realm of pure song" (CP, 172)—to be "released from the dreary dance of opposites" (CP, 173).

These thematics of the union of apparent opposites, the spirit's journey out of the self through regression into nature's small forms, the need to transcend rational understanding through leaps of imaginative vision and so forth, should by now be familiar enough to even those with a casual interest in Roethke's writing. What is equally important in "Meditations" is Roethke's movement into the American long-poem tradition of Whitman and Eliot. During the period of the composition and gestation of "Meditations," Roethke was influenced by his reading of S. Musgrove's critical study of the relation between Whitman's *Leaves of Grass* and Eliot's long poetry. "Meditations," as La Belle has shown, is shaped by the "stylistic parallels" linking Whitman and Eliot.[6] In particular, all three poets rely on repeated constructions at the beginning of line groups, technically called anaphora. Such anaphoric repetitions employ participial verbs, prepositional phrases, and infinitive sequences. These kinds of structures shape the "What is it to be a woman?" passage where Roethke uses repeated initial infinitives to multiply the possibilities of feminine experience:

> What is it to be a woman?
> To be contained, to be a vessel?
> To prefer a window to a door?
> A pool to a river? (CP, 169)

In these long meditative poems, Roethke also employs the kind of epic catalogues that Whitman uses to portray the rich democratic diversity of his expansive American long poem, *Leaves of Grass.* "Meditations" pioneers the verse forms and verbal techniques Roethke would go on to perfect in his last years. The poet's stylistic reliance on Whitman culminates in his posthumously published work "North American Sequence." Both poems anticipate the postwar revival of the American long-poem tradition of Whitman, Pound, Eliot, Crane, Stevens, and Williams. In particular, Roethke's late career looks forward to the long "projective" field poems of Charles Olson and Robert Duncan, the confessional long poems of John Berryman and W. D. Snodgrass, and the long surrealist and beat poems by Robert Bly, Allen Ginsberg, and Gary Snyder.

In addition to breaking new ground in the American long-poem tradition, *Words for the Wind* celebrates the poet's recent marriage by exploring the important motive of love as a symbol for the mystical fusion of secular and sacred experience. The volume presents both Platonic and erotic affirmations of the power of love in images of fire, air, and light. Beyond his idyllic love scenes, Roethke tests love's strength to endure the existential uncertainties of physical mortality, despair, and non-being in images that return to the dark subhuman world of his early and middle careers. Asserting the persistence of spiritual vision in the face of death is also the challenge Roethke takes up in "The Dying Man" and "Meditations of an Old Woman." This coming to terms with one's own finitude and affirming it as an ultimate truth becomes the thematic focus of the posthumous volume *The Far Field*.

Notes

1. Theodore Roethke, "Introduction to *Words for the Wind*," in *Poet's Choice*, ed. Paul Engle and Joseph Langland (New York: Dell, 1962) 99.

2. Engle and Langland 99.

3. Paul Tillich, *The Courage to Be* (London: Collins, 1952) 141–42. Cited by Parini 148; and by Malkoff 131.

4. Anthony Libby, "Roethke, Water Father," *American Literature* 46 (November 1974) 282.

5. From "Song of Myself," Walt Whitman, *Poetry and Prose* (New York: Library of America, 1982) 206 (hereafter cited in the text as CPW).

6. La Belle 128–30.

CHAPTER SIX

The Far Field:
"North American Sequence"

Composed just prior to the poet's death in 1963, Roethke's "North American Sequence" stands as his consummate celebration of American place. This magnum opus can be read as a counterpart to the inward garden world of the greenhouse poems, realizing the poet's quest for individuated dwelling in "The Lost Son." "North American Sequence" both regresses toward a deep communion with the life of things and elevates that strange witnessing into a unified aesthetic expression. Roethke personifies his completed vision in the central persona of "North American Sequence"—the "final man," or individuated self at one with the natural universe. The poet's career culminates in the movement beyond the lost son's anxious quest for identity to the self-reliance of the final man.

Stylistically, "North American Sequence" parts company with both the disruptive surrealism of the *Praise to the End!* sequence and the poetic formalism of *The Waking* and *Words for the Wind* in favor of long open forms. Whereas his early depiction of regional place is typically staged through a regressive flight from the language of High Modernist precursors, the portrayal of local landscape in "North American Sequence" enters into a more coherent dialogue with the poetry of Eliot, Stevens, and Yeats. Roethke replaces the truncated lines of "The Lost Son," that dramatize trauma and bewilderment, with longer more continuous line lengths conveying the fluid interchange of person and place. In particular, by using Whitman's patterns of repetition, anaphora, and catalogues in "Out of the Cradle Endlessly Rocking," Roethke explores the rhythms of dilation and contraction that rock between self and world, "In the cradle of all that is" (CP, 191). His final dialogue with poetic tradition translates the impersonal abstractions of Modernism into a more colloquial voice—one that meditates on the senses and significance of the contemporary American scene.

Lyric narration allows Roethke to abstract meaning from detailed explorations of place. But he also features language as event—as a verbal process that recovers nature's organic immediacy. The poet's descriptions exploit alliteration, consonance, onomatopoeia, and enjambment to voice words at one with the things they represent:

I live with the rocks, their weeds,
Their filmy fringes of green, their harsh
Edges, their holes
Cut by the sea-slime, far from the crash
Of the long swell,
The oily, tar-laden walls
Of the toppling waves,
Where the salmon ease their way into kelp beds,
And the sea rearranges itself among the small islands.
  (CP, 205)

In such performances, Roethke often recovers primal encounters with the world. Returning to the technique of the greenhouse poems, his poetry of natural disclosure focuses on the local textures and surfaces that have been touched and hollowed by the flux of reality's rearrangements. Roethke's monosyllabic diction presents American place through an austere speech hewn from language. His pattern of enjambment highlights the blossoming of a violent, imagistic aesthetic: "harsh / Edges," "holes / Cut," "crash / Of the long swell." In contrast, his final lengthening of the line provides a more expansive form for dispersing the compact tensions compressed into the shorter verses.

Beyond these stylistic techniques, Hugh Staples's musical analogy is helpful in understanding

NORTH AMERICAN SEQUENCE

the global structure of "North American Sequence" as evidenced in its first poem, "The Longing": "In a manner that suggests counter point in
music, the principle of alternation controls the
elaborate pattern of contrasting elements in the
poem: body and soul, the sense of self and the
release from subjectivity, earth and water, past and
present, motion and stasis. . . . The sequence,
then, can be regarded as a tone poem consisting of
an overture ("The Longing"), in which the major
themes appear, followed by four movements in
which the tensions and oppositions of the whole
sequence are summarized and move toward a
resolution."[1] "The Longing" not only anticipates
the poet's completed vision in "North American
Sequence," it opens as well onto the same landscapes of despair and turmoil that characterize the
earliest moments of the poet's career.

If the final man embodies the round of
Roethke's past poetic incarnations, then he must
also endure the returning moment of the lost son's
ennui. The organic mire of the greenhouse leaves
its residue in the rank physicality of "North American Sequence." In "The Longing" Roethke's
"kingdom of stinks and sighs, / Fetor of cock-
roaches, dead fish, petroleum" becomes both the
site for the poet's "Agony of crucifixion on
barstools" (CP, 187), and the portal opening onto

America's underworld of "sensual emptiness."
The final man claims America's "far field" by first
enduring the despair of its "bleak time" before
beholding the ecstasy of its "pure moment" (CP,
168). He commits himself to landscapes of interior
fatigue in "The Lost Son," now transplanted to the
exterior vistas of America's urban squalor:

> In a bleak time, when a week of rain is a year,
> The slag-heaps fume at the edge of the raw cities:
> The gulls wheel over their singular garbage;
> The great trees no longer shimmer;
> Not even the soot dances. (CP, 187)

The final man's patience defers the longing "to
transcend this sensual emptiness." When "the spirit
fails to move forward" (CP, 187), the poet becomes
versatile in his regressive identification with the
soul's "half-life"—the worm, slug, and other "eye-
less starers," whose blindness he shares in "The Lost
Son." Such descents into the chthonic underworld of
American place characterize Roethke's regressive
aesthetic: "I believe that the spiritual man must go
back in order to go forward" (PC, 12).

In the second section of "The Longing," to go
back is also to give up one's illusions based in
pride, hope, and fear: "A wretch needs his wretch-
edness. Yes. / O pride, thou art a plume on whose
head?" (CP, 188). That one pursues spiritual ful-

fillment, not in spite of the "sensual emptiness" of "things asleep," but through a deeper communion with nature's "nothings" is the central revelation of "The Longing":

> To this extent I'm a stalk.
> —How free; how all alone.
> Out of these nothings
> —All beginnings come. (CP, 188)

The final man's wisdom—his understanding that "the rose exceeds, the rose exceeds us all"—comes through radical self-abnegation that is "Bare as a bud, and naked as a worm" (CP, 188). Roethke draws out the paradox of this negative mysticism in his essay "On 'Identity'": "It is paradoxical that a very sharp sense of the being, the identity of some other being—and in some instances, even an inanimate thing—brings a corresponding heightening and awareness of one's own self, *and*, even more mysteriously, in some instances, a feeling of the oneness of the universe" (PC, 25). For Roethke, the consecration of nature's nothings into transfigured beginnings becomes a perpetual vocation. The final man's vision is expansive. His longing for "the beyond" propels him through nature's manifold creation. Being "beyond" is, paradoxically, to be fully present, to possess the identities of nature's prosaic nothings by voicing them anew:

"The light cries out, and I am there to hear— / I'd be beyond; I'd be beyond the moon, / Bare as a bud, and naked as a worm" (CP, 188).

Like Whitman, Roethke finds in the catalogue the central poetic vehicle for celebrating democratic openness. The catalogues and anaphora of "The Longing" gather the beginnings of American place into an expansive totality that finally becomes ecstatic in its attainment of the "beyond": "I would believe my pain: and the eye quiet on the growing rose; / I would delight in my hands, the branch singing, altering the excessive bird; / I long for the imperishable quiet at the heart of form" (CP, 188). Roethke finds the "redolent disorder of this mortal life" redemptive because it enables him to "unlearn the lingo of exasperation, all the distortions of malice and hatred" (CP, 188). That lingo is, in part, his former distortions of his precursor's language in "The Lost Son." Like that poem, "North American Sequence" enters into a dialogue with poetic tradition. But here the voices of the past no longer deny Roethke's literary identity. The imagery and form of "The Longing" emerge from the tension between, on the one hand, the poet's close attention to the life and identity of things, and on the other hand, his sensitivity to the rhetorical conventions of past writing. Specifically, Roethke achieves the beyond by first working his way through the presentation of landscape in past writing.

Roethke's imagination, for example, is profoundly shaped by his reading in English Romanticism, and as La Belle has shown, his vision of moonlight as a "great flame" rising "from the sunless sea" (CP, 188) echoes Coleridge's "Kubla Khan" and "Dejection, an Ode."[2] Roethke acknowledges that influence, however, to surpass it ultimately, thereby asserting a distinctively American poetic meditation beyond "the great dead." The final freedom, for Roethke, exists beyond the imaginative horizons established for him as a reader. For, as a writer he enters into a unique engagement with native place.

In section 3 of "The Longing" T. S. Eliot and Walt Whitman replace Coleridge as the poem's grounding in the form and diction of literary tradition. Several of Roethke's critics have identified the poem's final lines

> Old men should be explorers?
> I'll be an Indian.
> Ogalala?
> Iroquois (CP, 189)

as an allusion to Eliot's claim that "old men ought to be explorers" in part 5 of "East Coker" (CPE, 129). In Eliot's end is Roethke's beginning for he lives out Eliot's directive to enter into a deeper communion with the reality of the natural world. "The Longing" takes up Eliot's command to be "still and still moving" but abandons his meditation on a theological center of Christian authority. Roethke's longing for "the imperishable quiet at the heart of form" is just that—a longing, not an orthodoxy. For his part, Roethke abandons Eliot's "still center" of belief for the more existential immediacy of mortality's "redolent disorder."

Throughout "The Longing" Roethke adopts Eliot's role as explorer, but not so much in Christian terms. Instead, the poet commits himself to discovering images indigenous to the American Midwest and Northwest. Stylistically, Roethke abandons the formal, ruminative tones of Eliot's *Four Quartets* by adopting Whitman's more colloquial and democratic "breath unit" verse. In "Some Remarks on Rhythm" Roethke affirmed the contemporary revival of Whitman's prosody including the "breath unit, the language that is natural to the immediate thing, the particular emotion. . . . There are areas of experience in modern life that simply cannot be rendered by either the formal lyric or straight prose. We need the catalogue in our time" (PC, 83).

"Meditation at Oyster River" continues this poetic dialogue with Whitman. In diction and prosodic form, the poem speaks to Whitman's "Out of the Cradle Endlessly Rocking":

> Now, in this waning of light,
> I rock with the motion of morning;
> In the cradle of all that is,
> I'm lulled into half-sleep
> By the lapping of water,
> Cries of the sandpiper. (CP, 191)

Rocking between the Me and the Not-Me, Roethke adopts Whitman's meditative pattern of expansion toward and contraction from the otherness of nature. Stephen Whicher employs a binary system of "transcendental mode/demonic recessive" to describe Whitman's encounters with the Not-Me as a cycle of merging with and abandonment by the otherness of the natural world.[3] Like Whitman, Roethke depicts his own encounters with nature by shifting from first person narrative to more objective descriptions of place detailed in anaphoric catalogues. These shifts clearly inform Roethke's technique in "Meditation." Here he alternates descriptive portrayals of the Tittebawasee's tidal forces in sections 2 and 3 with first person narration in sections 1 and 4.

Moreover, Roethke follows Whitman's use of complementary paired images. In Whitman's poetry the major opposition of shore and surf denotes, according to Paul Fussel, Jr., "a reconciling of the 'simple separate person' with the 'En-Mass'; and finally . . . it can serve as a means of reconciling, without recourse to sacred history, love with loss, life with death, time with eternity."[4] Several of Roethke's critics have discussed such paired images in "North American Sequence": shadow/light, rock/wind, salt water/fresh water, rain/drought, calm/storm, and so forth.[5] These kinds of oppositions, as constituting metaphors, inform each poem of the group. Whereas poems such as "Meditation," "The Long Waters," and "The Rose" represent interior landscapes mainly through rivers, lakes, and tidal estuaries, Roethke's earth poems—"The Longing," "Journey to the Interior," and "The Far Field"—denote the objective, concrete locales of the American West and Midwest.

"Meditation" depicts a landscape of multiple reconciliations through the imagery of earth and water. Perched on "the low, barnacled, elephant-colored rocks" (CP, 190), the poet participates in the serene approach of the evening tide. Stylistically, he portrays the encroaching waves through participial verbs: "moving," "running," "creeping," and "slapping." Yet unlike his earlier use of participles to enact nature's storm in, say, "Big Wind," here the tranquil dusk offers "no violence." Instead, its calm flow moves toward the reconciling moment of communion between the Me and Not-Me. Roethke's meditative instant of intersection and transition is poised between day and night, shore and surf, light and darkness. The advent of evening is balanced in a calm center of stasis.

The dark night of section 2 offers the poet a paradoxical redemption. Although he must confront the otherness of the moon as "Death's face," paradoxically, it "rises afresh" (CP, 190). Its radiance persists beyond the "dying star" of the self in a collective dreamscape. Roethke swells his line here to catalogue Oyster River's elusive creatures. Intransitive verbs, participles, and verbal modifiers—"loping," "poised," "waiting," "whirring," "coming," "altered," "topped," "tugged," "rustling," "sliding," "creeping"—suggest the subtle diversity of the river's local settings.

Once again in section 3 Roethke asserts his longing for "a body with the motion of a soul" (CP, 188). Now "In this first heaven of knowing / The flesh takes on the pure poise of the spirit" (CP, 191). Roethke's celebration of incarnation expands outward through assuming the "sandpiper's insouciance / The hummingbird's surety, the kingfisher's cunning" (CP, 191). Moving from this quiet source of observation, "Meditation" assumes a mounting imaginative crescendo. Specifically, the force of Roethke's water musings gathers momentum—from the "first trembling of a Michigan brook in April" to the "wrist-thick cascade tumbling from a cleft rock" (CP, 191)—climaxing in a famous passage that describes the breaking up of the ice-bound Tittebawasee "in the time between winter and spring":

And the midchannel begins cracking and heaving
    from the pressure beneath,
The ice piling high against the iron-bound spiles,
Gleaming, freezing hard again, creaking at midnight—
And I long for the blast of dynamite,
The sudden sucking roar as the culvert loosens its de-
    bris of branches and sticks,
Welter of tin cans, pails, old bird nests, a child's shoe
    riding a log,
As the piled ice breaks away from the battered spiles,
And the whole river begins to move forward, its
    bridges shaking. (CP, 191)

These memorable lines dramatize the poet's awed witnessing of the river's natural spectacle through onomatopoetic participles: "cracking," "heaving," "piling," "gleaming," "freezing," "shaking." The poem's depiction of the absurd "welter" of things thrown into bizarre juxtaposition presents an original rendering of regional place—one that rivals the example of Whitman. Roethke's masterful orchestration of the flood tide achieves a verbal power that exceeds the mere imitation of Whitman's poetic language and style. Only through this violent fragmentation of nature, paradoxically, can Roethke enter "the cradle of all that is" (CP, 191).

Section 4 shifts from Roethke's earlier descriptions to a narrative mode that witnesses to the midpoint of dusk whose in-between time balances two temporal orders. Although Roethke sits in the "waning of light," he anticipates the dawn, where, he says, "I rock with the motion of morning" (CP, 191). Having communed with his native land in language, the poet can be rocked out of the self into nature's cradle. The poem's "half-sleep" mediates dark and light, self and world, life and death. At the close of "Meditation" the poet focuses on the shorebird's amphibious dwelling as another metaphor for his own mystical fusion of earth and water, life and death, the secular life of natural things and the eternally sacred. Like the sandpiper, the poet negotiates "the edge" mediating contrarieties with an easy and graceful versatility:

Water's my will, and my way,
And the spirit runs, intermittently,
In and out of the small waves,
Runs with the intrepid shorebirds—
How graceful the small before danger! (CP, 191–92)

THE FAR FIELD

"Journey to the Interior" furthers Roethke's aesthetic of risk, that becomes "graceful . . . before danger." "Journey" reclaims the fluid communion of "Oyster River" with nature now through an arduous passage inland. Employing the metaphor of the car trip, Roethke dramatizes his risky traversal of "the edge" of death's austere boundaries. Once again he endures the lost son's traumatic quest for the final man's interior mastery:

> In the long journey out of the self,
> There are many detours, washed-out interrupted
>   raw places
> Where the shale slides dangerously
> And the back wheels hang almost over the edge
> At the sudden veering, the moment of turning.
>   (CP, 193)

In an earlier poem from *Open House*, "Highway: Michigan," Roethke depicts the road's traffic from a pastoral vantage point, viewing it as the "progress of the jaded." From this ideal perspective he reduces America's highway to a demonic version of Whitman's open road, portraying it as an emblem of contemporary America's dehumanizing mass industrialization. There Roethke's commuters are "the prisoners of speed" addicted to the momentary thrill the highway offers. "Acceleration is their need," but final escape from "What their hands have made" happens only through tragedy:

NORTH AMERICAN SEQUENCE

"One driver, pinned beneath the seat, / Escapes from the machine at last" (CP, 33). But the mature poet in "Journey to the Interior" jettisons these kinds of pastoral moral tags. Instead, Roethke seeks an aesthetic redemption, paradoxically, by more deeply identifying with America's brutal machinery.

In "Journey" the poet boldly asserts the road as symbol for one of his major poetic themes: "the means of establishing a personal identity" out of "the chaos of modern life" (PC, 19). Acceleration dramatically serves the poet's need for ecstatic immanence. Roethke's detour onto America's "washed out interrupted raw places" provides the dramatic occasion for aesthetic fulfillment. Similar to his fascination with the Tittebawasee's brute power, Roethke finds an exhilarating tension in the road's constant potential for violence. "At the sudden veering, the moment of turning," the poet must "hug close" (CP, 193) to the moment's edge of peril. This risk lends a visceral suspense to Roethke's poetics of immediacy.

The poet's affirmative union with the road's machine becomes ecstatic in section 2 of "Journey." Asserting a kind of intuitive correspondence between the outer highway and the inner, spiritual path, the poet opens a way through nature's mortal scene. Roethke's journey achieves a violent mobility through the poet's surrender to the road's chance terrain. But through this risk he realizes a moment of dynamic control. Self and landscape interpenetrate in the "deep pit at the bottom of the swale" (CP, 193) and then thrust forward toward a climactic fusion. Roethke tests his will against the resistance of the physical world in a consummate moment of survival. As driver, Roethke discovers a grace before danger in the "long moment" centered in a vision of survival and mastery:

> And the sun comes out of a blue cloud over the
> Tetons,
> While, farther away, the heat-lightning flashes.
> I rise and fall in the slow sea of a grassy plain,
> The wind veering the car slightly to the right,
> Whipping the line of white laundry, bending the
> cottonwoods apart,
> The scraggly wind-break of a dusty ranch-house.
> I rise and fall, and time folds
> Into a long moment. (CP, 194)

For Richard Allen Blessing, this passage "speeds into the eternal present," that he compares to Eliot's intersection of secular time with eternity.[6] Yet Blessing's comparison somewhat exceeds Roethke's more contingent act of centering.

Although Eliot's appeal to the "still" transcendence of Christian Incarnation resembles the "long moment" depicted in "North American Se-

quence," Roethke's centering is a more existential
act. His long moment neither transcends its
grounding in local place nor points to an ideal core
of universal truth. Instead, out of the focused
possession of place nature speaks to the poet
through its indigenous plants and animals:

> And I hear the lichen speak,
> And the ivy advance with its white lizard feet—
> On the shimmering road,
> On the dusty detour. (CP, 194)

Only the "dusty detour" out of the self will bring
Roethke face to face with the *logos* of things themselves.

Having survived the encounter with rural
America in sections 1 and 2, the poet enters in
section 3 the wider unconscious domain of the
collective self. Here Roethke returns to the fluid
water landscapes of "Oyster River." With the transition to evening, "Journey" shifts from the violent
inland traveling of the day to the interior passage
through sleep and dream. Earlier, the surrealistic
landscapes of "The Lost Son" had enacted
Roethke's regressive flight from his poetic fathers.
Now in "North American Sequence" Roethke asserts his own poetic identity in marked stylistic
contrast to the early discontinuous and truncated
lines of "The Lost Son." The last lines of "Journey"

summarize the poet's final reconciliation to his literary tradition: "The spirit of wrath becomes the spirit of blessing, / And the dead begin from their dark to sing in my sleep" (CP, 195).

The dead in this context are Eliot, Whitman, and Yeats, and they appear not as the menacing father figures that haunt "The Lost Son," but as familiar echoes that the poet attends to and engages in dialogue. The probable source for Roethke's meditation on the relationships among death, dreaming, and poetry is Yeats's idea of the "complementary dream" which, as Helen Vendler describes it, mediates between the living and dead through art: "The term 'Complementary Dream' (which Yeats later abandoned) suggests strongly the reciprocal relation between human art and the 'life' of the 'dead.'. . . The 'dead' dream about human life, reliving it; the living, when they produce art, are incarnating a dream about the life in the world of the dead."[7]

Moreover, by transplanting the writing of Eliot, Whitman, and Yeats into the local landscape of American place, Roethke renovates their poetry in a more contemporary verbal performance. Grafting his diction onto the roots of "Out of the Cradle Endlessly Rocking" Roethke adopts Whitman's rocking motion between shore and surf, self and world, leading to "The soul at a still-stand, / At

ease after rocking the flesh to sleep" (CP, 194).
"Journey" also echoes the intersection of time and
the timeless in the imagery of Eliot's *Four Quartets*,
particularly "Burnt Norton." Roethke's lines

In the moment of time when the small drop forms,
   but does not fall,
I have known the heart of the sun,—
In the dark and light of a dry place,
In a flicker of fire brisked by a dusty wind (CP, 191)

in tone, rhythm, and imagery invoke "the still
point of the turning world," "the moment in and
out of time," that Eliot portrays in both the drained
pool at Chipping Campden, and the "flicker" of
light in the tube-station of "Burnt Norton" (CPE,
120). The moment of intersection, which Roethke
views in "the heart of the sun," also recalls Eliot's
"heart of light" (CPE, 118) in the rose garden of
"Burnt Norton" as well as his encounter with the
"hyacinth girl" of *The Waste Land* (CPE, 38). The
mediation of light and dust returns to the moment
in "Burnt Norton" "Between un-being and
being. / Sudden in a shaft of sunlight / Even while
the dust moves" (CPE, 122). Similarly, when
Roethke visualizes the unity of space and time as
"the flower of all water, above and below me, the
never receding, / Moving, unmoving in a parched
land, white in the moonlight: / The soul at a still-

stand" (CP, 194), he recalls Eliot's correspondent
"white light still and moving" (CPE, 119). As in his
earlier dialogues with Eliot (in "The Longing" and
"Journey," part 2), Roethke limits his investments
in ideal, universal truths. Instead, he substitutes
the immediacy of his poetic vision for Modernism's
appeals to transcendent authority.

In addition to his use of Whitman's and Eliot's
earth, water, and light imagery, Roethke also employs Yeatsian fire and air motifs to enact his
"complementary dream." In "Byzantium" a celestial, insubstantial flame cleanses "at midnight"
"the unpurged images of day," while the "blood-
begotten spirits" and the crowing of a fabled
golden bird dispel the secular sounds of "the
Emperor's drunken soldiery" (YVE, 497). In
Roethke's poem the condition of fire, the "flicker of
fire" introduced in stanza 2, also appears in conjunction with "A slight song / After the midnight
cries" (CP, 194). Although these lines echo Yeats's
poem, Roethke prunes his writing of Yeats's more
elaborate symbolism. In contrast, Roethke locates
"the slight song" of native place in the spontaneous "drip of leaves." Roethke features Yeats's
iconography of mediation even more explicitly in
stanza 3. Here Roethke directs the incarnate world
of day toward the collective nightlife of the imaginative "dead":

NORTH AMERICAN SEQUENCE

I rehearse myself for this:
The stand at the stretch in the face of death,
Delighting in surface change, the glitter of light on
    waves,
And I roam elsewhere, my body thinking,
Turning toward the other side of light,
In a tower of wind, a tree idling in air,
Beyond my own echo (CP, 194–95)

Roethke's sense of his poetic vocation as a re-
hearsed performance adopts Yeats's stance of
achieving unity with an aesthetic mask—the poet's
personified opposite—at the extreme moment of
death. Roethke further grounds his text within
Yeats's characteristic imagery of "unified being."
Roethke's "tower of wind" recalls the tower to
which the primary soul summons the antithetical
self in Yeats's "Dialogue of Self and Soul."
Roethke's tower, looming on "the other side of
light," echoes Yeats's "The Tower" where the poet
asserts death as an imaginative construct and
counterpart to life that the dead "Dream and so
create / Translunar Paradise" (YVE, 415). Yeats
portrays the imagination's power to create illusion
through the figure of the blind poet Homer whose
mythic portrayal of Helen's beauty "all living
hearts betrayed." Yeats's blind poet, whose art
would make moonlight and sunlight seem "one
inextricable beam" (YVE, 411), finds his counter-

part in Roethke's final man who affirms spiritual insight as a kind of blindness to the world:

As a blind man, lifting a curtain, knows it is morning,
I know this change:
On one side of silence there is no smile;
But when I breathe with the birds,
The spirit of wrath becomes the spirit of blessing,
And the dead begin from their dark to sing in my
    sleep. (CP, 195)

At the close of "Journey" both Roethke's diction (blessing) and imagery (the poem's "tree idling in air") recall Yeats's "Vacillation." The first moment of ecstasy, that for Roethke exists "Beyond my own echo / Neither forward nor backward, / Unperplexed, in a place leading nowhere" (CP, 195), is similar to Yeats's stance in "Vacillation" "Between extremities (YVE, 499). The ecstatic transfiguration of "blessing" corresponds to Yeats's similar experience of momentary epiphany in section 4 of "Vacillation": "It seemed, so great my happiness,/ That I was blessed and could bless" (YVE, 501). In "Journey" Roethke reduces his precursors' desire for transcendent truth to his more immediate and existential communion with the immediacy of regional place. His dialogue with the "great dead" of literary tradition balances the scenic presentation of American landscape in sections 1 and 2 with a more verbal terrain of past writing in section 3.

NORTH AMERICAN SEQUENCE

As traveler and poet, Roethke journeys toward a double identity that centers him, finally, both within the immediacy of nature and amongst his poetic "ancestors."

Having sung with the "dead" in the final stanzas of "Journey," Roethke returns to the daylight world of local place in "The Long Waters." Section 1 grounds the poet in a typically American locale "Where the fresh and salt waters meet, / And the sea-winds move through the pine trees, / A country of bays and inlets, and small streams flowing seaward" (CP, 196). "The Long Waters" focuses on the beauty of local textures— the way in which "bunched logs peel in the afternoon sunlight," or how "yellowish prongs of grass poke through the blackened ash" (CP, 196).

In section 2, Roethke avoids reality's inundating tide that he had earlier suffered in "The kingdom of bang and blab" in "The Lost Son." His invocation to Blake's Mnetha, Mother of Har, protects him from "the dubious sea-change, the heaving sands" (CP, 196). Ultimately, Roethke's final man overcomes the recollected fear of nature's flux endured in "The Lost Son." Now, he can invoke nature as muse:

But what of her?—
Who magnifies the morning with her eyes,
That star winking beyond itself,

THE FAR FIELD

The cricket-voice deep in the midnight field,
The blue jay rasping from the stunted pine. (CP, 196)

Roethke's personification of nature as muse leads the poet from the celestial beyond ("that star winking beyond itself") down into the "deep" organic realm of sensual desire. The poet descends, as in the previous poems of "North American Sequence," through death—toward "the dry bloom" and "first snow" of late autumn. Roethke affirms his passage into "the dark fir" forest in spite of a poignant intuition that time will foreshorten his poetic career: "Feeling, I still delight in my last fall" (CP, 197).

A landscape of ecological transition stages the final man's meditation on the relation of time and death to imaginative vision: "In time when the trout and young salmon leap for the low-flying insects, / And the ivy-branch, cast to the ground, puts down roots into the sawdust" (CP, 197). As an exemplary scene of survival, the tidal estuary reconciles death and life in time. In "The Long Waters" each instant of life shares in a moment of death, and vice versa, decay is creation. The trout, young salmon, and osprey as predators share in a dynamic network of fleshly transfiguration. Similarly, the ivy branch "cast to the ground . . . puts down roots" for new growth, while the sinking pine tilted toward death nevertheless provides a nest for the osprey. Even in this swamp of mortality, Roethke takes note of the subtle balance of life and death. Nature's floral abundance everywhere dispels the despair of time's mutability. Roethke's botanical catalogue—lily, mottled tiger, heliotrope, morning-glory, and burdock—resists the depth of symbolic meaning. Instead, the poet celebrates the common ground nurturing all life: "Down by the muck shrinking to the alkaline center" (CP, 197). Stanza 2 advances the poem's scenic descent toward the sea. Employing oxymoron, the rhetorical yoking of opposites, Roethke portrays this fusion as a "rich desolation . . . where salt water is freshened / By small streams running down under fallen fir trees" (CP, 197).

Section 4 shifts from this descriptive landscape to an internalized water world that resonates with the wave patterns of the collective self developed through narration in "Meditation at Oyster River." Again Roethke witnesses the "one long undulant ripple," here a "single wave," that in the poet's simile becomes endlessly refracted by cross-winds. The stillness of centered vision, or long moment achieved in the midst of "Journey"'s violent immediacy, returns in "The Long Waters" in the figure of the "stone breaking the eddying current." Roethke's stone is anchored in "the dead middle

THE FAR FIELD

way, / Where impulse no longer dictates, nor the darkening shadow" (CP, 197).

Section 5 fuses the objective rendering of place with the poet's subjective meditation. Stanza 1 presents a series of almost epic similes that describe the final man's identity in terms of nature's collective body. The closing narrative utterances of "The Long Waters" celebrate Roethke's ultimate possession as final man—his vision of the self's incarnate confluence with the American landscape:

I see in the advancing and retreating waters
The shape that came from my sleep, weeping:
The eternal one, the child, the swaying vine branch,
The numinous ring around the opening flower,
The friend that runs before me on the windy head-
    lands,
Neither voice nor vision. (CP, 198)

"The numinous ring around the opening flower" as a kind of imaginative intelligence graces nature with its ecstatic power. Having mastered the violent passage through the American west in "Journey to the Interior," Roethke now discovers himself at one with the strange presence he has summoned from "the advancing and retreating waters" of the North American coast. This sudden communion allies the poet to the redemptive fellowship of the "far field," which he here depicts as "The friend that runs before me on the windy headlands, / Neither voice nor vision." The final man's voice comes "back from the depths laughing too loudly" and ranges out "beyond the farthest bloom of the waves" (CP, 198). Roethke uses an imagistic language to evoke nature's contingent flux and encompassing narrative maxims to abstract meaning from immediate experience. In this poem, as in "Journey," Roethke's depiction of place fuses the locales of waking reality and dream. "The Far Field" becomes yet another site where conscious and unconscious images are "gathered together" for the individuated self.

In "The Far Field" Roethke resumes his car trip, venturing ever inward through the dark tunnel of the self. Yet unlike "Journey to the Interior" he abandons his energetic, and even playful, taunting of death. Now the enervating winter season stalls Roethke's momentum and leaves him to the nightmare of America's "washed out, interrupted raw places." The journey out of the self toward death takes the poet to "the field's end" in section 2 where Roethke, like the lost son, confronts the debris of the American waste land. Yet it is, paradoxically, in the graveyard of "tin cans, tires, rusted pipes, broken machinery," Roethke says, that "One learned of the eternal" (CP, 199). The final man only enters the redemptive horizon of the far field by first communing with what were once the necessary allies of the lost son's "hard time": the rat, catbird, and field mouse. Roethke accepts the visceral brutality of the American scene, embodied here in the tom-cat's "entrails strewn over the half-grown flowers, / Blasted to death by the night watchman" (CP, 199). The rehearsal for "The stand at the stretch in the face of death" (CP, 194) that Roethke practiced in "Journey" and "The Long Waters" serves him now in the movement beyond death's finality. Images of motion and energetic change replace death's stasis and stagnation in the final man's celebration of spring: "I suffered for birds, for young rabbits caught in the mower, / My grief was not excessive. / For to come upon warblers in early May / Was to forget time and death" (CP, 199).

As in "Oyster River," Roethke again conveys the elusive gestures of nature's creatures through participial verbs. Whether "moving" or "hanging," the spontaneous life of Roethke's "bird shapes,— / Cape May, Blackburnian, Cerulean," is "fearless" and so teaches the poet "to forget time and death." The "deep" identification with nature's evolution, which the lost son experiences as a baptism in "River Incident" returns here with the final man's déjà vu and anticipation of future incarnation:

NORTH AMERICAN SEQUENCE

—Or to lie naked in sand,
In the silted shallows of a slow river,
Fingering a shell,
Thinking:
Once I was something like this, mindless,
Or perhaps with another mind, less peculiar;
Or to sink down to the hips in a mossy quagmire;
Or, with skinny knees, to sit astride a wet log,
Believing:
I'll return again,
As a snake or a raucous bird,
Or, with luck, as a lion. (CP, 200)

Roethke's meditation, his "thinking" and "believing," projects outward through a pattern of anaphoric conjunctions that multiply the possibilities of being. The varied line length, that contracts and expands with the rhythms of the poet's musings, stands as a visual counterpart to Roethke's credo that "to go forward as a spiritual man it is necessary first to go back" (PC, 39). As in the other poems of this sequence, Roethke here juxtaposes descriptive catalogues of nature's beginnings with more narrative stanzas that abstract from nature the global significance of metempsychosis:

I learned not to fear infinity,
The far field, the windy cliffs of forever,
The dying of time in the white light of
tomorrow,

THE FAR FIELD

> The wheel turning away from itself,
> The sprawl of the wave,
> The on-coming water. (CP, 200)

The poet's characteristic images: "the far field," "the dying of time in the white light of tomorrow," "the sprawl of the wave," and "on-coming water" reverberate with the larger constituting metaphors of "North American Sequence." In contrast to the insular dwelling of the lost son, the final man can survive the open-ended vistas of the American scene. By fully realizing his poetic vocation in this sequence, Roethke claims the democratic infinitude of the American continent as his imaginative territory.

Section 3 returns to the landscape of convergences, to "a country half land, half water" (CP, 201). The poet's commitment to concrete perception allows him to affirm in the final stanza of section 3: "I am renewed by death, thought of my own death," because "What I love is near at hand, / Always, in earth and air" (CP, 201). The fourth section of "The Far Field" stands as a transitional bridge to "The Rose." Here the final man personifies the sequence's major themes, representing the individuated self. Roy Harvey Pearce points to the final man as one of "two grand efforts toward synthesis in 'The Far Field'."[8] Roethke's final man is versatile in negotiating nature's flux.

NORTH AMERICAN SEQUENCE

Because he can merge with the far field of his
imaginings, he completes the tentative immersions
in the collective landscapes of "The Lost Son":
"The lost self changes / Turning toward the
sea, / A sea-shape turning around" (CP, 201).
Roethke's final man is expansive and generates
from his imaginative center the world he comes to
inhabit:

> A man faced with his own immensity
> Wakes all the waves, all their loose wandering fire.
> The murmur of the absolute, the why
> Of being born fails on his naked ears. (CP, 201)

Richard Allen Blessing associates the final man
with the "philosopher's man" of Stevens's "Asides
on the Oboe."[9] Like Stevens's "central man,"
Roethke's final man embodies "the end of all
things." The globe of his knowing is the plenitude
of "finite things" that together "reveal infinitude."
Listening to the "murmur of the absolute," the
final man becomes wholly transparent. "His spirit
moves," Roethke writes, "like monumental wind"
(CP, 201).

Stanza 3 catalogues the recollected settings
and concrete perceptions that make up the "serene
of memory in one man":

> The mountain with its singular bright shade
> Like the blue shine on freshly frozen snow,

THE FAR FIELD

> The after-light upon ice-burdened pines;
> Odor of basswood on a mountain-slope,
> A scent beloved of bees;
> Silence of water above a sunken tree. (CP, 201)

Roethke's communion with "the blue shine on freshly frozen snow" does not ascend toward the bright summits of absolute truth, as in the Romantic tradition, but fades into the darkness of water, submergence, and death in the image of a sunken tree. For Roethke, only this regressive descent toward memory rooted in native place leads to a progressive expansion "Winding around the waters of the world" (CP, 201).

"The Rose," the final poem of "North American Sequence," gathers together the poet's major constituting metaphors and motives into a symphonic coda, celebrating the final man's individuated consciousness. Section 1 reaffirms Roethke's commitment to the American landscape by focusing again on the tidal estuary of "The Long Waters": "There are those to whom place is unimportant, / But this place, where sea and fresh waters meet / Is important" (CP, 202). Twilight returns the poet to the temporal in-between time of "Meditation at Oyster River." Again Roethke employs participial verbs and the catalogue to describe the intersection of afternoon and evening. Roethke witnesses the departure of the "morning birds . . . twittering finches . . . / The last geese crossing against the reflected afterlight" (CP, 202). Gradually the echoing "cries of the owl, the eerie whooper" give way to the silence of evening and its "lessening waves." This confluence of air, fire, and water imagery provides the setting for the merging of various opposites: day/night, ego/collective self, and life/death.

The third stanza's meditative, narrative language recapitulates the interior night journey of "Meditation" section 2, "Journey" section 3, "The Long Waters" section 5, and "The Far Field" section 3. Twilight commences the ecstatic journey into the sequence's long waters, where Roethke writes, "I sway outside myself . . . / Into the small spillage of driftwood" (CP, 202). Participial verbs again describe the dynamic "flowering and widening" of his organic symbol of "the wild sea rose" struggling to "gather together" the natural landscape. As in previous movements of "North American Sequence," Roethke here moves "beyond," paradoxically, through a deeper regressive identification with the lowly and primordial dwellers of nature's dark lagoons. This section culminates in Roethke's doubling of the present's "sea-rose" with the recollected garden world of "The Lost Son":

And I think of roses, roses,
White and red, in the wide six-hundred-foot
   greenhouses,

THE FAR FIELD

And my father standing astride the cement benches,
Lifting me high over the four-foot stems, the Mrs.
    Russells, and his own elaborate hybrids,
And how those flowerheads seemed to flow toward
    me, to beckon me, only a child, out of myself.
    (CP, 203)

Unlike Romantic reminiscences on childhood, such
as Wordsworth's "Ode: Intimations of Immortality," Roethke does not heighten his recollected
youth with an ideal, spiritual landscape. Instead,
his floral revery focuses on the greenhouses'
earthy realism. Roethke's prosaic memories offer a
contemporary alternative to Romantic poems of
recollected youth based on a Platonic heaven of
ideal forms: "What need for heaven, then, / With
that man, and those roses?" (CP, 203).

In "The Rose" Roethke becomes "that man,"
the final man, by passing beyond the greenhouse
enclosures of "The Lost Son" and into the expansive domain of America's "far field." By giving
voice to the "sound and silence" of regional place,
Roethke's vision becomes openly democratic, identifying with his audience now through the collective pronoun "us": "What do they tell us, sound
and silence?" (CP, 204). What "American sounds"
tell us, for Roethke, are their identities. The poet's
catalogue of his nation's native voices—thrush,

NORTH AMERICAN SEQUENCE

killdeer, catbird, bobolink—blend with the more
evanescent noise of things themselves:

> The bluebird, lover of holes in old wood, lilting its
>   light song,
> And that thin cry, like a needle piercing the ear, the
>   insistent cicada,
> And the ticking of snow around oil drums in the
>   Dakotas,
> The thin whine of telephone wires in the wind of a
>   Michigan winter. (CP, 204)

In section 3 Roethke gathers together America's "ample geography" into a subtle listening to

> That single sound,
> When the mind remembers all,
> And gently the light enters the sleeping soul,
> A sound so thin it could not woo a bird,
> Beautiful my desire, and the place of my desire.
>   (CP, 204)

Roethke's emphasis on the individual, the final
man, at the center of the democratic whole returns
to Whitman's stress on the value of the individual
self as a counterpart to America's infinite vistas:
"This second principle," writes Whitman, "is individuality, the pride and centripetal isolation of a
human being in himself—identity—personalism.
. . . This is the thought of identity—yours for you,
whoever you are, as mine for me" (CPW, 958, 960).

THE FAR FIELD

For both Whitman and Roethke, the final man or self's vision achieves an expansive encounter with democratic openness, yet it voices a wholly personal song. The particular personality of the "Me" provides the center of identity that, as Whitman says, is the "only entrance to all facts" (CPW, 960). Roethke's grounding in a deep sensitivity to place and his own individuality allows him to go beyond what Whitman indicts as the "creeds" and "conventions" of past literary traditions. The final stanzas of "The Rose" provide a thematic summary of Roethke's central revelation as the final man. Here he affirms the paradoxical mystery of incarnation. To achieve, as he says, "the true ease of myself" is to step "outside myself, / Beyond becoming and perishing, / A something wholly other." This otherness is at once mobile and centered: "As if I swayed out on the wildest wave alive, / And yet was still" (CP, 205). Throughout "The Rose" the poet negotiates this central paradox.

Roethke's characteristic pastoral settings, regional locales, imagery, central motives, and rhetorical styles all culminate in the aesthetic unity of "North American Sequence." Here Roethke achieves a constituting form for celebrating a lifetime's engagement with poetry. His strategy features images at once gleaned from the immediacy of regional America and internalized "Beyond becoming and perishing" in the final man's "calm center" of poetic vision. "North American Sequence" also presents a sustained dialogue with the poet's literary tradition. In particular, Roethke's revision of High Modernism translates its ironic, self-reflexive aesthetic into a more democratic and colloquial performance. In this way, he realizes a poetics of what Yeats describes as "unity of being," even as he embraces the expansive diversity of America's democratic horizon.

Notes

1. Hugh B. Staples, "The Rose in the Sea-Wind: A Reading of Theodore Roethke's 'North American Sequence,'" *American Literature* 36, (May 1964) 192–93.

2. La Belle 152.

3. Stephen Whicher, "Whitman's Awakening to Death," in *The Presence of Walt Whitman*, ed. R. W. B. Lewis (New York: Columbia University Press, 1962) 6.

4. Paul Fussel, Jr., "Whitman's Curious Warble: Reminiscence and Reconciliation," in *Lewis* 32.

5. See Rosemary Sullivan, *Theodore Roethke the Garden Master* (Seattle, WA: University of Washington Press, 1975) 162; and Denis Donoghue, "Theodore Roethke's Broken Music," in Stein, Essays on the Poetry 152–53.

6. Richard Allen Blessing, *Theodore Roethke's Dynamic Vision* (Bloomington, IN: Indiana University Press, 1974) 143.

7. Helen Hennessy Vendler, *Yeats's Vision and the Later Plays* (Cambridge: Harvard University Press, 1963) 84.

8. Roy Harvey Pearce, "Theodore Roethke: The Power of Sympathy," in Stein, *Essays on the Poetry*, 193.

9. Blessing 153.

CHAPTER SEVEN

The Far Field: "Love Poems," "Mixed Sequence," and "Sequence, Sometimes Metaphysical"

Published posthumously, the "Love Poems," and "Mixed Sequence" of *The Far Field* are generally considered as more uneven poetic performances than "Sequence, Sometimes Metaphysical"—a collection published during the poet's life. Several of Roethke's short love lyrics lack the power and originality of those collected in *Words for the Wind.* They frequently lapse into mannered and formulaic recapitulations of earlier subjects, themes, imagery, motives, and stylistic conventions. "Her Time," for example, recalls the language of stillness from "Journey to the Interior." In the former poem we find the poet "In the time / When the tide moves / Neither forward nor back" (CP, 210), whereas in "Journey" Roethke also moves "Neither forward nor backward / Unperplexed, in a place leading nowhere" (CP, 195). Similarly, the imagery of "the edge," that the poet fails to achieve in "Song"—"My wrath, where's the edge /

Of the fine shapely thought" (CP, 211)—recalls
"The Shape of the Fire" where "The edge cannot
eat the center" (CP, 63) and "In a Dark Time,"
where the poet claims that "The edge is what I
have" (CP, 239). "Her Longing," likewise, seems a
somewhat less powerful version of Roethke's "The
Longing" of "North American Sequence." The
centrifugal spiritual direction of Roethke's persona—"perpetually rising," as she says, "out of
myself" (CP, 209)—resembles the motion of "The
Rose" where the poet writes "I sway outside
myself / Into the darkening currents" (CP, 202).
Moreover, the erotic lyricism of "Light Listened"
recalls Roethke's passionate love poem "I Knew a
Woman." But "Light Listened" lacks the rich,
metaphysical coupling of body and mind that
Roethke earlier portrayed in strikingly sensual imagery.

The figure of the lover in "The Happy Three"
and "Her Wrath" is reduced to a domestic carica-
ture: "Inside, my darling wife / Sharpened a
butcher knife; / Sighed out her pure relief / That I
was gone" (CP, 213). "Wish for a Young Wife,"
however, tempers love's failures in marriage with a
wise forgiveness. Here Roethke attempts to rein-
vest the realities of fallen experience with an ideal
innocence in order to achieve what Blake would
describe as an "organized innocence":

THE FAR FIELD

My lizard, my lively writher,
May your limbs never wither,
May the eyes in your face
Survive the green ice
Of envy's mean gaze;
May you live out your life
Without hate, without grief,
And your hair ever blaze,
In the sun, in the sun,
When I am undone,
When I am no one. (CP, 217)

Significantly, Roethke bestows his advice to the "Young Wife" from the vantage point of the final man's wisdom that is enlightened by the knowledge of death's imminence. Beyond such love poems, with the exception of works such as "The Abyss" and "The Storm" that both introduce fresh images and striking maxims into the Roethke canon, *The Far Field's* next section is as the title intimates a "mixed" performance.

William Heyen has cogently argued in "The Divine Abyss: Theodore Roethke's Mysticism," that the poet "dramatizes, for an age that has lost its faith, an individual's hard and dark mystic way to God, whose essence he best perceives when he descends into and experiences the true nature of the Divine Abyss."[1] In an age of agnosticism, the terms of transcendence in "The Abyss" initially take the form of the very impossibility of belief. The poem's five-part structure, as Heyen and others have argued, is loosely based on the five stages of mystical experience outlined in Underhill's comprehensive work *Mysticism*. Like Yeats, Underhill was a student of Baron Friedrich von Hügel, thus making her an even more attractive source for Roethke's thoughts on spirituality. As early as 1946, Roethke recorded her scheme for mystical experience almost verbatim into his notebooks:

1) Awakening—to a sense of divine reality.
2) Purgation of self, when it realizes its own (unprojecting) divine.
3) An enhanced return to the sense of the divine order, after the Self has achieved its detachment from the world.
4) Dark night of the Soul.

Singleness: Discovery of the self is the same as discovery of God in oneself.[2]

The poem opens with a traditional image of mystical descent—the staircase icon of St. John of the Cross:

> And the abyss? the abyss?
> "The abyss you can't miss:
> It's right where you are—
> A step down the stair." (CP, 219)

THE FAR FIELD

The poem's pattern of questions, that border on nonsense rhymes, replicates the sense of bewildered confusion that overtakes "The Lost Son." Moreover, the empty house imagery of "Open House" and "The Lost Son" returns here as a symbol of despair:

> Each time ever
> There always is
> Noon of failure,
> Part of a house. (CP, 219)

Awakening to the Divine, initially, is an unsettling, traumatic recognition of the self's secular failures that in section 2 leads to the need for purgation: "I have been spoken to variously / But heard little," the poet confesses, "I have taken, too often, the dangerous path, / The vague, the arid, / Neither in nor out of this life" (CP, 220). The soul's arid, dangerous path recalls Eliot's scenic imagery of spiritual dessication in the fifth section, "What the Thunder Said," of *The Waste Land*.

In negotiating the journey out of the self, once again the poet descends into the chaotic psychic landscapes of "The Lost Son"—the "kingdom of bang and blab" (CP, 54). Here he invokes Whitman's expansive openness to experience enumerated through his anaphoric catalogues: "Be with me Whitman, maker of catalogues: / For the

MIXED SEQUENCE

world invades me again / And once more the tongues begin babbling" (CP, 220). Detachment from the world and return to divine order happen in section 3 as a further estrangement, as a "surfeit" or excess of "immediacy": "Too much reality can be a dazzle, a surfeit; / Too close immediacy an exhaustion" (CP, 220). As Neil Bowers has argued, Roethke's depiction of the transcendent moment, as a "fearful instant" that can "Strike like a fire" (CP, 221), parallels the *Noche Escura del Alma* or "dark night of the soul" of St. John of the Cross, explicated in Underhill's *Mysticism*:

The self is in the dark because it is blinded by a Light greater than it can bear—that "Divine Wisdom which is not only night and darkness to the soul, but pain and torment too." "The more clear the light, the more does it blind the eyes of the owl, and the more we try to look at the sun the feebler grows our sight and the more our weak eyes are darkened. So the divine light of contemplation, when it beats on the soul not yet perfectly purified, fills it with spiritual darkness, not only because of its brilliance, but because it paralyzes the natural perception of the soul."[3]

Section 4 describes the self's separation from God in the long dark night of the soul. Assailed by doubts, the poet questions whether his progress toward God is genuine or merely an imaginative fiction: "Do we move toward God," he asks, "or merely another condition?" (CP, 221). But the very despair of the abyss's skeptical unease, where the soul is fated to "rock between dark and dark" (CP, 221), serves as the necessary precondition for the poet's merging with the "luminous stillness" praised in the fifth and final section of "The Abyss." In the poem's idiom, "knowing" the Eternal begins and emerges out of, paradoxically, the state of "not-knowing" (CP, 221). Disclosures of the Divine, in other words, happen initially as a process of obscuring spirituality. Again, the probable source for Roethke's presentation of mystical experience here, according to Neal Bowers, is Evelyn Underhill's reading of an anonymous fourteenth-century work *The Cloud of Unknowing:* "This darkness and this cloud is, howsoever thou dost, betwixt thee and thy God, and letteth thee, that thou mayest neither see Him clearly by light of understanding in thy reason, nor feel Him in sweetness of love in thine affection."[4]

As is often the case in Roethke's writing, the union with divine presence joins natural to transcendental dwelling, thereby enabling the poet to "hear the flowers drinking in their light" and to take "counsel of the crab and the sea-urchin" (CP, 222). The soul's bonding to God is also depicted in the traditional Christian imagery of marriage. "I am," the poet says, "most immoderately married"

MIXED SEQUENCE

(CP, 222). Roethke's eclectic presentation of spiritual awakening here also draws from the Buddhist tradition through the image of the bo-tree, where the Buddha is reputed to have received enlightenment. Furthermore, Roethke's line "Being, not doing, is my first joy" (CP, 222) reflects the passivity of Buddhism's goal of achieving a meditative identification with the void of nirvana. The poet's overcoming of the mutable world of secular change—of becoming—as Underhill affirms, is the traditional aim of all mystical heritages: "Being," she says, "not Doing, is the first aim of the mystic."[5]

Lesser companion-pieces to Roethke's meditations on the abyss of mortality in "Mixed Sequence" include "Elegy" and "Otto." Roethke's elegiac recollections of his deceased Aunt Tilly resemble such earlier musings on feminine personae as the greenhouse "witches" of "Frau Bauman, Frau Schmidt, and Frau Schwartze." All these figures appear as one with the earthy settings they nurture. An unconscious borrowing Roethke employs in his description of Aunt Tilly's "face like a rain-beaten stone," as La Belle has shown, derives from Yeats's same image in "The Magi": "their ancient faces like rain-beaten stones" (YVE, 318).[6] In a contemporary parody of Yeats's numinous invocation of the dead, Roethke envisions her

> . . . in some celestial supermarket,
> Moving serenely among the leaks and cabbages,
> Probing the squash,
> Bearing down, with two steady eyes,
> On the quaking butcher. (CP, 223)

"Otto" is another filial poem that ruminates on the shaping influence Roethke's father exerted over the poet's career. This poem registers calmer and more mature tones than a work like "The Lost Son." Nevertheless, there is a poignant undercurrent that emerges in the final stanza, as the poet once again recalls the approach of "papa":

> The long pipes knocked: it was the end of night.
> I'd stand upon my bed, a sleepless child
> Watching the waking of my father's world.—
> O world so far away! O my lost world! (CP, 225)

"The Lizard" and "The Meadow Mouse" comprise short vignettes depicting Roethke's close attention to nature's tiny lives. Roethke's poetic eye for the particular, argues La Belle, is influenced by the detailed imagistic portraits of flora and fauna in D. H. Lawrence's *Birds*, *Beasts*, *and Flowers*: "Roethke learned from Lawrence," she writes, "how to make the reader forget the poet entirely and see only the creature."[7] The poet's short lyric "The Manifestation" sums up this poetics of natural creation: "Many arrivals make us live: the tree becoming / Green, a bird tipping the topmost bough, / A seed pushing beyond itself, / The mole making its way through darkest ground" (CP, 235). In "The Tranced," however, Roethke turns beyond the subterranean, subhuman world of worm and mole. "We struggled out of sensuality," he writes, ". . . Our eyes fixed on a point of light so fine / Subject and object sang and danced as one" (CP, 237). These latter two poems depart from the imagistic textures of Roethke's earlier nature poems. Instead, they return to the poetry of meditative and abstract statement that predominates in "Sequence, Sometimes Metaphysical," and the compressed lyric utterances of "In a Dark Time," in particular.

Roethke claimed that "In a Dark Time" came to him, like his formalist lyric "The Dance," almost spontaneously with very little need for revision. Several of his critics, however, question the poem's almost automatic composition because it is carefully structured in the same five stages of mystical revelation Roethke studied in Underhill. In any case, Roethke's masterful compression of themes and images into tight stanzas of iambic pentameter encapsulates his major concerns in a masterful verbal performance that eludes the mannered style of his other late works.

The opening stanza, like that of "The Wak-

THE FAR FIELD

ing," presents an inaugural moment of the soul's turn toward spiritual vision. This initial insight is staged through the same paradoxical blending of opposites that shapes Roethke's mystical vision throughout his career: "In a dark time, the eye begins to see" (CP, 239). The psychic correspondence between the soul's insight and nature's subhuman forms is depicted in Jungian terms as the poet's encounter with his shadow, a figure for all those aspects of the self that are normally unconscious to it: "I meet my shadow in the deepening shade; / I hear my echo in the echoing wood— / A lord of nature weeping to a tree" (CP, 239). Neal Bowers argues that this last line looks backward to Roethke's first manic episode in which he claimed to have had an experience of mystical oneness with a tree.[8] This seems a plausible reading given that the stanza concludes with the poet's reawakening to his sympathy with "Beasts of the hill and serpents of the den"—again merging scenic opposites of hill and den.

Stanza 2 dramatizes the moment of purgation as a kind of madness that tests the soul through a fiery rite of passage. Roethke's definition of madness as the "nobility of soul / At odds with circumstance" recalls Wallace Steven's definition of poetic nobility in *The Necessary Angel* as an imaginative violence that presses back against the chaotic violence of material circumstances.[9] Here the shadow's progress reaches the dead end of "pure despair," where it is "pinned against the sweating wall" much as Prufrock is "pinned and wriggling on the wall" in "The Love Song of J. Alfred Prufrock" (CPE, 5). But teasing out the "winding path" "among the rocks"—here the traditional locale of spiritual testing as in Satan's taunting of Christ in the wilderness—leads to Roethke's affirmation that "The edge is what I have" (CP, 239). Throughout his career, Roethke thrived on risk, pushing his personal and professional lives to the uttermost extremities of what he could possibly endure. Writing served as whetstone for honing the edge of the poet's experience. This lived intensity, as Kenneth Burke has observed, lends his strongest verse an aura of dramatic suspense. Roethke's poems "about the edge of Revelation," says Burke, ". . . suggest a state of vigil, the hope of getting the girl, of getting a medal, of seeing God."[10] For his part, Roethke viewed the "edge" as a kind of psychic threshold or border among shifting mental states and phenomena. To master the edge, he said, is to possess "The feeling that one is on the edge of many things: that there are many worlds from which we are separated by only a film; that a flick of the wrist, a turn of the body

THE FAR FIELD

another way will bring us to a new world" (SF, 147).

Stanza 3 celebrates the achieved illumination of "A steady storm of correspondences" (CP, 239) between self and nature. Death of the old ego leads, as in the *Praise to the End!* sequence, to a transfigured, albeit uncanny, witnessing of the spirit's incarnation in the physical world: "Death of the self in a long, tearless night, / All natural shapes blazing unnatural light" (CP, 239). The poem's last stanza comprises the final two stages of the poet's mystical transactions with the Divine: the dark night of the soul followed by ecstatic illumination. Evelyn Underhill describes the dark night as "the last painful break with the life of illusion, the tearing away of the self from that World of Becoming in which all its natural affections and desires are rooted, to which all its intellect and senses correspond; and the thrusting of it into that world of Being where at first, weak and blinded, it can but find a wilderness, a 'dark'."[11] The dark night culminates in a demonic simile in stanza 4 identifying the soul with "some heat-maddened summer fly"—a traditional reminder of the body's mortality. This estranging moment climaxes in Roethke's bewildered question "Which I is I? leading to the poet's movement beyond despair into unity: "A fallen man, I climb out of my

fear" (CP, 239). The mind's contact with the Divine
in the poem's final couplet dramatically rips it out
of the secular world of becoming into the "tearing
wind" of the "One" of being. Roethke's paradoxical understanding of unity again recalls W. B.
Yeats. Specifically, the severing away of the secular
self as an initiatory rite of passage to the One
echoes "Crazy Jane Talks with the Bishop," where
Yeats writes "For nothing can be sole or whole /
That has not been rent" (YVE, 513).

The remaining lyrics of "Sequence, Sometimes
Metaphysical" continue to probe the darkness of
the human condition, but only occasionally arriving at the affirmative spiritual unity that "In a Dark
Time" realizes. "In Evening Air" is a reminiscence
on how the poet once "transcended time" but the
poem stalls in Roethke's final witnessing to "How
slowly dark comes down on what we do" (CP,
240). As an arresting coda to "In a Dark Time,"
"The Sequel" presents an unsettling moment of
reflection and doubt that questions the authenticity
of metaphysical vision. The poet wonders, "Was I
too glib about eternal things?" (CP, 241). The
second stanza aims to reclaim the oneness of
being, returning to the imagery of "The Dance,"
but Roethke loses the edge of his poetry's usual
dramatic force in a somewhat redundant and mannered recycling of the earlier piece: "We danced,

we danced, under a dancing moon; / And on the coming of the outrageous dawn, / We danced together, we danced on and on" (CP, 241). The poem ends, as in "In Evening Air," with the failure of light, moving into an all-enveloping scenic darkness, figured in the traditional association of death with the autumnal season: "I feel the autumn fail— all that slow fire / Denied in me, who has denied desire" (CP, 242). "Infirmity," as the title implies, presents a prolonged rumination on and complaint about the body's physical mortality. Here we find the poet "dying inward, like an aging tree" (CP, 244). The sequence's theme of the need for spiritual vision in the face of death is repeated in a reductive version of "In a Dark Time." Returning to the theme of unifying antitheses, Roethke employs the figures of synaesthesia, the blending of the senses, and chiasmus, a rhetorical crossing of sight and hearing: "When opposites come suddenly in place, / I teach my eyes to hear, my ears to see" (CP, 244). Similarly, "The Marrow" begins with the image of the fly as a metaphor for spiritual darkness, employed in stanza 4 of "In a Dark Time": "The wind from off the sea says nothing new. / The mist above me sings with its small flies" (CP, 246). Like the uncertain, skeptical questioning of "The Sequel," Roethke is once more possessed

by doubts about the endurance of God in an age of
agnosticism.

In one of his journal entries Roethke playfully
speculated that "If we think long enough about
God, we may create Him" (SF, 225). Following
Paul Tillich, Roethke questions whether the eternal
oneness of being persists beyond our representa-
tions or icons of the Divine: "Godhead above my
God," he asks, "are you there still?" In addition,
the poet admits to the abyss of the soul's dark
night separating it from God: "From me to Thee's
a long and terrible way" (CP, 246). The poem, of
course, can offer no easy resolution to the "terrible" gulf distancing the self from God, and
Roethke resists any casual or glib celebrations of
"external things" (CP, 241). The movement of
these lyrics taken together does risk such celebrations, however, in essentially the same images that
characterize mystic illumination throughout
Roethke's career. Again in "The Tree, The Bird"
the dark night of the soul gives way to the
"pure . . . motion of the rising day" (CP, 248)
where later the poet in "The Restored" "danced, at
high noon / . . . In the still point of light" (CP, 249)
or as he repeats the same idea in somewhat dif-
ferent terms in "Once More, the Round": "And
everything comes to One / As we dance on, dance
on, dance on" (CP, 251).

THE FAR FIELD

Beyond the mannered recapitulations of earlier works, the strong poetry of Roethke's late canon can be credited with bridging the Modernist and Postmodernist periods. Like Eliot, Roethke's poetics of the abyss plumbs the existential despair inaugurated by the proclamation of God's death in Nietzsche's *The Gay Science.* Roethke viewed himself as one of the twentieth-century's "hollow men" and survived. Learning from Stevens that "Death is the mother of beauty, mystical,"[12] Roethke overcame nihilism hearkening back to earlier, pre-Modern celebrations of what William Heyen terms the "Divine Abyss." In his last poems, Roethke viewed himself as at once a "Child of the dark" (CP, 250) and a "self-enchanted man" (CP, 248). He had the spiritual courage to ask such ultimate questions as "Godhead above my God, are you there still?" (CP, 246). Moreover, he possessed the imaginative strength to endure the unsettling knowledge of such questioning, understanding that "Eternity's not easily come by" (CP, 244). Although his presentations of spiritual destitution look forward to the lyric explorations of nothingness and non-being in W. S. Merwin and James Wright, Roethke's special talent for depicting the dance of nature's redemptive immanence also anticipates the Postmodern animism of poets such as Robert Bly and James Dickey. Roethke

endured an apocalyptic epoch where, as he says,
"The edge of heaven was sharper than a sword;
/ Divinity itself malign, absurd" (CP, 237). Yet even
now his poetic vision transfigures "The dire dimension of a final thing" (CP, 248), pointing the
way to luminous moments of what Dickey describes as "pure being."[13]

Notes

1. William Heyen, "The Divine Abyss: Theodore Roethke's
Mysticism," *Texas Studies in Literature and Language* 11 (Winter 1969)
1068.

2. Theodore Roethke, "Teaching Notes," 6 April 1946. Cited in
Parini 135–36.

3. Underhill 399; cited in Bowers 174.

4. Underhill 350; cited in Bowers 175.

5. Underhill 380; cited in Bowers 176.

6. La Belle 143.

7. La Belle 146.

8. Bowers 182.

9. See Wallace Stevens, "The Noble Rider and the Sound of
Words" 35.

10. Burke 105.

11. Underhill as cited in Parini 178.

12. Wallace Stevens, *The Palm at the End of the Mind,* ed. Holly
Stevens (New York: Alfred A. Knopf, 1971) 7.

13. Dickey 220.

BIBLIOGRAPHY

Primary Sources—Books

Open House. New York: Alfred A. Knopf, 1941.

The Lost Son and Other Poems. Garden City, NY: Doubleday, 1948; London: John Lehmann, 1949.

Praise to the End!. Garden City, NY: Doubleday, 1951.

The Waking: Poems 1933–1953. Garden City, NY: Doubleday, 1953.

The Exorcism: A Portfolio of Poems. San Francisco, CA: Mallette Dean, 1957. A limited edition of 1150 copies.

Words for the Wind. London: Secker and Warburg, 1957; Garden City, NY: Doubleday, 1958; Bloomington, IN: Indiana University Press, 1961.

I AM! Says the Lamb. Garden City, NY: Doubleday, 1961. With drawings by Robert Ledenfrost.

Party at the Zoo. New York: Crowell-Collier Modern Masters Book for Children, 1963. Illustrated by Al Swiller.

Sequence, Sometimes Metaphysical. Iowa City, IA: Stone Wall Press 1963. Limited edition of 330 copies; with wood engravings by John Roy.

The Far Field. Garden City, NY: Doubleday, 1964; London: Faber and Faber, 1965.

On the Poet and His Craft: Selected Prose of Theodore Roethke, ed. Ralph J. Mills, Jr. Seattle, WA: University of Washington Press, 1965.

The Collected Poems of Theodore Roethke. Garden City, NY: Doubleday, 1966; London: Faber, 1968; Doubleday/ Anchor, 1975; University of Washington Press, 1982.

Selected Letters of Theodore Roethke, Ed. Ralph J. Mills, Jr. Seat-

BIBLIOGRAPHY

tle, WA: University of Washington Press, 1968; London: Faber, 1970.

Selected Poems of Theodore Roethke. Ed. Beatrice Roethke. London: Faber, 1969.

Straw for the Fire: From the Notebooks of Theodore Roethke, 1943–63. Ed. David Wagoner. Garden City, NY: Doubleday, 1972.

Dirty Dinky and Other Creatures: Poems for Children. Ed. Beatrice Roethke and Stephen Lushington. Garden City, NY: Doubleday, 1973.

Primary Sources—Selected Essays and Nonfiction

"Open Letter." *Mid-Century American Poets.* Ed. John Ciardi. New York: Twayne Publishers, 1950. 67–72. Reprinted in *On the Poet and His Craft.* 36–43.

"An American Poet Introduces Himself and His Poems." BBC Broadcast, July 30, 1953 Disc SLO 34254. Reprinted in *On the Poet and His Craft.* 7–13.

"Theodore Roethke." *Twentieth Century Authors, First Supplement.* Ed. Stanley J. Kunitz. New York: H. W. Wilson, 1955. 837–38. Reprinted in *On the Poet and His Craft.* 14–17.

"How to Write Like Somebody Else." *Yale Review* 48 (March 1959): 336–43. Reprinted in *On the Poet and His Craft.* 61–70.

"Some Remarks on Rhythm." *Poetry* 97 (October 1960): 35–46. Reprinted in *On the Poet and His Craft.* 71–84.

"Theodore Roethke—Comment." *The Contemporary Poet as Artist and Critic.* Ed. Anthony Ostroff. Boston: Little, Brown, 1964. 49–53.

"Introduction to *Words for the Wind.*" *Poet's Choice.* Ed. Paul Engle and Joseph T. Langland. New York: Dial Press, 1962. 96–100.

BIBLIOGRAPHY

"On 'Identity'," as part of "Roethke Remembered." *Show* 5 (May 1965): 11–12, 15. Reprinted in *On the Poet and His Craft*. 18–27.

Concordance and Bibliographies

Lane, Gary, ed. *A Concordance to the Poems of Theodore Roethke*. Metuchen, NJ: Scarecrow Press, 1972.

McLeod, James R. *Theodore Roethke: A Manuscript Checklist*. Kent, OH: Kent State University Press, 1971.

Moul, Keith R. *Theodore Roethke's Career: An Annotated Bibliography*. Boston: G. K. Hall, 1977.

Secondary Sources—Books

Blessing, Richard Allen. *Theodore Roethke's Dynamic Vision*. Bloomington, IN: Indiana University Press, 1974. Blessing's study benefits from the use of Roethke's notebooks to analyze the poet's early growth, middle career, and final vision.

Bowers, Neal. *Theodore Roethke: The Journey from I to Otherwise*. Columbia, MO: University of Missouri Press, 1982. Bowers argues that Roethke's recurrent incidents of manic-depression provided the poet with irrational and mystical subjects for his verse.

Chaney Norman. *Theodore Roethke: The Poetics of Wonder*. Washington, DC: The University Press of America, 1981. Chaney examines Roethke's place in the context of both intellectual history and his legacy.

Foster, Ann T. *Theodore Roethke's Meditative Sequences: Contemplation and the Creative Process*. Studies in Art and Religious Interpretation. Vol. 4. Lewiston, NY: E. Mellen, 1985. Arguing that Roethke is essentially a religious poet, Foster, like Bowers, draws out the connection between Roethke's mystical meditations and his poetics.

BIBLIOGRAPHY

Heyen, William, ed. *Profile of Theodore Roethke*. Columbus, OH: Charles E. Merrill, 1971. Heyen's volume is a useful compilation of previously published works by such critics as Kenneth Burke, John Ciardi, David Ferry, Stanley Kunitz, Jerome Mazzaro, James McMichael, Delmore Schwartz, and Allan Seager.

La Belle, Jenijoy. *The Echoing Wood of Theodore Roethke*. Princeton, NJ: Princeton University Press, 1976. La Belle presents a detailed influence study of Roethke's sources.

Malkoff, Karl. *Theodore Roethke: An Introduction to the Poetry*. New York: Columbia University Press, 1966. Malkoff's study remains a touchstone for later critics in his defense of Roethke's nonsense verse, his focus on the poet's psychological themes, and general overview of the "organic growth of his work."

Martz, William J. *The Achievement of Theodore Roethke*. Glenview, Ill.: Scott, Foresman, 1966. Martz's early study locates Roethke in the Romantic tradition and probes the issue of the poet's relation to "that tradition in terms of his own *originality*."

Mills, Ralph J., Jr. *Theodore Roethke*. Minneapolis: University of Minnesota Press, 1963. The first book on Roethke, Mills's study provides a comprehensive overview of the poet's career in terms of the self's spiritual journey.

Parini, Jay. *Theodore Roethke: An American Romantic*. Amherst, MA: University of Massachusetts Press, 1979. As his title implies, Parini views Roethke as an heir to the tradition of Coleridge, Emerson, Whitman, Wordsworth, and German Romanticism.

Rodgers, Audrey. *The Universal Drum: Dance Imagery in the Poetry of Eliot, Crane, Roethke, and Williams*. University Park, PA: Pennsylvania State University Press, 1979. Rodgers explores dance as a constituting metaphor for

BIBLIOGRAPHY

"kinetic activity," ineffable experience, myth and ritual, and "transcendent" experience.

Ross-Bryant, Lynn. *Theodore Roethke: Poetry of the Earth, Poet of the Spirit*. National University Publications. Port Washington, NY: Kennikat Press, 1981. Ross-Bryant reads Roethke's career in terms of the structural "circularity" of organic patterns and cycles of growth.

Stein, Arnold, ed. *Theodore Roethke: Essays on the Poetry*. Seattle, WA: University of Washington Press, 1965. Still the definitive collection on Roethke, this volume comprises articles by Donoghue, Hoffman, Martz, Mills, Pearce, Snodgrass, Spender, and Wain, among others.

Stiffler, Randall. *Theodore Roethke, The Poet and His Critics*. Chicago, IL: American Library Association, 1986. Stiffler provides a comprehensive reading of the critical reception of Roethke's major volumes through the early 1980s.

Sullivan, Rosemary. *Theodore Roethke: The Garden Master*. Seattle, WA: University of Washington Press, 1975. Emphasizing themes of self and environment, Sullivan uses the poet's letters and notebooks to explore the themes of love, death, and God.

Williams, Harry. *"The Edge is What I Have": Theodore Roethke and After*. Lewisburg, PA: Bucknell University Press, 1977. Williams provides a brief overview of Roethke criticism through the mid-1970s. He offers close readings of the major long poems and a final discussion of Roethke's influence on later contemporary figures.

Wolff, George. *Theodore Roethke*. Boston: Twayne Publishers, 1981. Wolff's study offers a useful introductory overview of the development and shape of the poet's career, and of the major works in the Roethke canon.

BIBLIOGRAPHY

Biography
Secondary Sources—Periodicals and Compilations

Seager, Allan. *The Glass House: The Life of Theodore Roethke.*
New York: McGraw-Hill, 1968. Seager's book still stands
as the definitive biography of Roethke, following the
course of the poet's life from his Saginaw childhood
through his academic career and his emergence and
growth as a major American poet.

Bogen, Don. "Intuition and Craftsmanship: Theodore
Roethke at Work." *Papers on Language and Literature* 18
(Winter 1982): 58–76. Using the more than 250 notebooks
Roethke accumulated between 1930–63, Bogen focuses on
the process of editing and refinement to which Roethke
submitted his "deep" image poetry in *Praise to the End!*
———. "From *Open House* to the Greenhouse: Theodore
Roethke's Poetic Breakthrough." *Journal of English Literary
History* 47 (Summer 1980): 399–418.

Bowers, Neal. "Theodore Roethke: The Manic Vision." *Modern Poetry Studies* 11 (1982): 152–63. Bowers offers detailed
documentation from the poet's notebooks of the connection between Roethke's "manic depressive syndrome" and
his interest in mysticism.

Bowers, Susan. "The Explorer's Rose: Theodore Roethke's
Mystical Symbol." *Concerning Poetry* 13 (Fall 1980): 41–49.
Exploring the difference between Roethke's pioneering
exploration of the American wilderness in "North American Sequence" and the earlier motive of the garden world,
Bowers focuses on the wild rose as a culminating emblem
for Roethke's late sequence.

Burke, Kenneth. "The Vegetal Radicalism of Theodore
Roethke." *Sewanee Review* 58 (Winter 1950): 68–108. Re-

BIBLIOGRAPHY

printed in *Profile of Theodore Roethke*, 19–46. One of the first major treatments of Roethke's aesthetic as developed in *The Lost Son.* Burke focuses on the thematics of regression, the idea of the "edge" of the poet's visionary intensity, and the rhetoric and surrealistic imagery of Roethke's psychological poetics.

Dickey, James. "The Greatest American Poet." *Atlantic* 222 (November 1968): 53–58. Reprinted in *Sorties: Journals and New Essays.* Garden City, NY: Doubleday, 1971. 214–24. Dickey's review of Allan Seager's *The Glass House* examines Roethke's biographical personae and emphasizes themes of embodied experience and the importance of local place.

Donoghue, Denis. "Theodore Roethke." *Connoisseurs of Chaos: Ideas of Order in Modern American Poetry.* New York: Macmillan, 1965. 216–45. Reprinted as "Roethke's Broken Music" in *Theodore Roethke: Essays on the Poetry.* 136–66. Donoghue argues for the mixed success of Roethke's integration of influences: Eliot, Hopkins, Joyce, Stevens, and Yeats.

Freer, Coburn. "Theodore Roethke's Love Poetry." *Northwest Review* 11 (Summer 1971): 42–66. Freer charts Roethke's theme of love as it progresses from secular to sacred experience.

Heyen, William. "The Divine Abyss: Theodore Roethke's Mysticism." *Texas Studies in Literature and Language* 11 (Summer 1969): 1051–68. Reprinted in *Profile of Theodore Roethke.* 100–16. Heyen adapts Evelyn Underhill's five-stage format of mystical knowledge to a close reading of Roethke's "The Abyss."

Hoffman, Frederick J. "Theodore Roethke: The Poetic Shape of Death." *Theodore Roethke: Essays on the Poetry.* 94–114. Reprinted in *Modern American Poetry.* Ed. Jerome Mazzaro.

BIBLIOGRAPHY

New York: David McKay, 1970. 301–20. Hoffman's study charts Roethke's poetics through four stages: from "prenatal condition to childhood, to the move toward maturity, and to the contemplation of the conditions and implications of death."

Kizer, Carolyn. "Poetry: School of the Pacific Northwest." *New Republic* 135 (16 July 1956): 18–19. Kizer provides insight into Roethke's methods as a teacher of and poetic mentor for the Pacific Northwest school of poets at the University of Washington.

Kunitz, Stanley. "Roethke: Poet of Transformations." *New Republic* 152 (23 January 1965): 23–29. Reprinted in *Profile of Theodore Roethke*, 67–77. Kunitz describes Roethke's verse in terms of the "shape-shifters who turn into the protagonists of his poems."

Libby, Anthony. "Roethke, Water Father." *American Literature* 46 (November 1974): 267–88. Reprinted in *Mythologies of Nothing: Mystical Death in American Poetry, 1940–70.* Urbana, IL: University of Illinois Press, 1982. 101–25. Libby considers Roethke to be a "seminal voice in contemporary poetry" and traces his influence on ephebes of the 1960s.

Martz, Louis L. "Theodore Roethke: A Greenhouse Eden." *The Poem of the Mind: Essays on Poetry, English and American* New York: Oxford University Press, 1966. 162–82. Reprinted from "A Greenhouse Eden." *Theodore Roethke: Essays on the Poetry*, 14–35. Martz argues that Roethke's strongest work is *The Lost Son,* claiming that the meditative style of the greenhouse poems constitutes "one of the permanent achievements of modern poetry."

Mazzaro, Jerome. "Theodore Roethke and the Failures of Language." *Modern Poetry Studies* 1 (July 1970): 73–96. Reprinted in *Profile of Theodore Roethke*, 47–64; and *Postmodern American Poetry.* Urbana, IL: University of Illinois Press,

BIBLIOGRAPHY

1980. 59–84. Mazzaro explores the issues of linguistic experimentation and influence in the poetry. He defends Roethke against the charge of "ventriloquism" arguing that his eclectic style "enables the poet to tap and channel an energy that depth psychologists claim is American."

McMichael, James. "The Poetry of Theodore Roethke." *The Southern Review* 5 (Winter 1969): 4–25. Reprinted in *Profile of Theodore Roethke.* 78–95. Considering Roethke's progress through the journey motif, McMichael provides a close reading of "North American Sequence."

Meredith, William. "A Steady Storm of Correspondences: Theodore Roethke's Long Journey Out of the Self." *Shenandoah* 16 (Autumn 1964): 41–54. Reprinted in *Theodore Roethke: Essays on the Poetry.* 36–53. Meredith focuses on the *Praise to the End!* sequence as central to the Roethke canon.

Mills, Ralph J., Jr. "In the Way of Becoming: Roethke's Last Poems." *Theodore Roethke: Essays on the Poetry,* 115–35. Mills argues here for Roethke's last poems as the climax of his poetic talents.

———. "Theodore Roethke: The Lyric of the Self." *Poets in Progress: Critical Prefaces to Ten Contemporary American Poets,* ed. Edward B. Hungerford. Evanston, IL: Northwestern University Press, 1962. 3–23. Mills argues that of all the postwar poets Roethke has "demonstrated the most restless and exploratory impulse."

Nelson, Cary. "The Field Where Water Flowers: Theodore Roethke's 'North American Sequence.' " *Our Last First Poets.* Urbana, IL: University of Illinois Press, 1981. 31–62. Nelson defends the poet's late career by examining his mediating role between the "introspective values" of the greenhouse poems and the expansive challenge of American place and its cultural history.

BIBLIOGRAPHY

Ostroff, Anthony, ed. "The Poet and His Critics: A Sympo-
sium." *The Contemporary Poet as Artist and Critic*. Boston:
Little, Brown. 1964. The symposium comprises readings of
"In a Dark Time" by John Crowe Ransom (26–35), Babette
Deutsch (36–40), and Stanley Kunitz (41–48).

Parini, Jay. "Blake and Roethke: When Everything Comes to
One." *Blake and the Moderns*, ed. Robert J. Bertholf and
Annette S. Levitt. Albany, NY: State University of New
York Press, 1982. 73–91. Parini provides a detailed exami-
nation of Blake's mythic influences on Roethke's imagina-
tion throughout his career.

Pearce, Roy Harvey. "Theodore Roethke: The Power of
Sympathy." *Theodore Roethke: Essays on the Poetry*, 167–99.
Pearce traces the theme of "sympathy" through all of
Roethke's major volumes.

Schwartz, Delmore. "The Cunning and the Craft of the Unconscious and the Preconscious." *Poetry* 94 (June 1959):
203–205. Reprinted in *Profile of Theodore Roethke*, 64–66.
Schwartz provides an early reading of Roethke's presentation of the unconscious through a poetics that extends
Yeat's Modernist style.

Scott, Nathan A., Jr. "The Example of Roethke." *The Wild
Prayer of Longing: Poetry and the Sacred*. New Haven, CT:
Yale University Press, 1971. 76–118. Scott provides a reading of Roethke's "sacramental vision" throughout his major volumes and offers a cogent account of Roethke's
understanding of piety.

Snodgrass, W. D. " 'That Anguish of Concreteness'—
Theodore Roethke's Career." *Theodore Roethke: Essays on
the Poetry*. 78–93. Snodgrass argues for a decline in
Roethke's poetic powers after *The Lost Son* and *Praise to the
End!* volumes.

Spanier, Sandra Whipple. "The Unity of the Greenhouse

BIBLIOGRAPHY

Sequence: Roethke's Portrait of the Artist." *Concerning Poetry* 12 (Spring 1979): 53–60. Spanier reads the sequence allegorically in terms of both the poet's chronological movement through birth, survival, growth, death, and eternity on the one hand, and his process of artistic creation on the other hand.

Spender, Stephen. "The Objective Ego." *Theodore Roethke: Essays on the Poetry.* 3–13. The term "objective ego" derives from Rimbaud's "objective poetry." Spender employs it as a rubric for the self's identification with "surrounding objects."

Staples, Hugh. "The Rose in the Sea Wind: A Reading of Theodore Roethke's 'North American Sequence'." *American Literature* 36 (May 1964): 189–203. Comparing Roethke's long sequence with Eliot's *Four Quartets,* Staples argues for the epic expansion of Roethke's earlier spiritual quest.

Van Dyne, Susan R. "Self Poesis in Roethke's 'The Shape of the Fire'." *Modern Poetry Studies* 10 (1981): 121–35. Van Dyne reads "The Shape of the Fire" as a transitional but central work reviewing motifs in *The Lost Son* and looking forward to the style, rhetoric, themes, and images of *Praise to the End!.*

Vernon, John. "Theodore Roethke's *Praise to the End!* Poems." *The Iowa Review* 2 (Fall 1971): 60–79. Reprinted as "Theodore Roethke." *The Garden and the Map: Schizophrenia in Twentieth-Century Literature and Culture.* Urbana, IL: University of Illinois Press, 1973. 159–90. Vernon offers a comprehensive analysis of the themes, imagery, ironic paradoxes, and ambiguities that together describe a world that eludes "the dualistic structures of classical Western thought."

BIBLIOGRAPHY

John Wain. "Theodore Roethke." *Critical Quarterly* 6 (Winter 1964): 322–38. Reprinted as "The Monocle of My Sea-Faced Uncle" in *Theodore Roethke: Essays on the Poetry*. 54–77. Wain emphasizes Roethke's poetry of the body as it leads to spiritual knowledge. He criticizes, however, the lack of social experience in Roethke's work.

INDEX

INDEX

INDEX

INDEX

INDEX

INDEX

INDEX

INDEX

INDEX